AF609466

Contents

1

State at a Glance

Uttarakhand , officially the State of Uttarakhand, formerly known as Uttaranchal, is a state in the northern part of India. It is often referred to as the *Devbhumi* (literally "Land of the Gods") due to a large number of Hindu templesand pilgrimage centres found throughout the state. Uttarakhand is known for the natural environment of the Himalayas, the Bhabharand the Terai. On 9 November 2000, Uttarakhand became the 27th state of the Republic of India, being created from the Himalayan and adjoining northwestern districts of Uttar Pradesh. It borders Tibet to the north; the Sudurpashchim Pradesh of Nepal to the east; the Indian states of Uttar Pradesh to the south and Himachal Pradesh to the west and north-west as well as Haryana on its south-western corner. The state is divided into two divisions, Garhwal and Kumaon, with a total of 13 districts. The interim capital of Uttarakhand is Dehradun, the largest city of the state, which is a railhead. The High Court of the state is located in Nainital.

Archaeological evidence supports the existence of humans in the region since prehistoric times. The region formed a part of the Kuru and the Panchal kingdoms (*mahajanpads*) during the Vedic age of Ancient India. Among the first major dynasties of Kumaon were the Kunindas in the 2nd century BCE who practised an early form of Shaivism. Ashokan edicts at Kalsi show the early presence of Buddhism in this region. During the medieval period, the region was consolidated under the Kumaon Kingdom and Garhwal Kingdom. In 1816, most of modern Uttarakhand was ceded to the British as part of the Treaty of Sugauli. Although the erstwhile hill kingdoms of Garhwal and Kumaon were traditional rivals, the proximity of different neighboring ethnic groups and the inseparable and complementary nature of their geography, economy, culture, language, and traditions created strong bonds between the two regions which further strengthened during the Uttarakhand movement for statehood in the 1990s.

The natives of the state are generally called Uttarakhandi, or more specifically either Garhwali or Kumaoni by their region of origin. According to the 2011 Census of India, Uttarakhand has a population of 10,086,292, making it the 20th most populous state in India.

Etymology

Uttarakhand's name is derived from the Sanskrit words *uttara* (M0) meaning 'north', and *khand* meaning 'land', altogether simply meaning 'Northern Land'. The name finds mention in early Hindu scriptures as the combined region of "Kedarkhand" (present day Garhwal) and "Manaskhand" (present day Kumaon). Uttarakhand was also the ancient Puranic term for the central stretch of the Indian Himalayas.

However, the region was given the name *Uttaranchal* by the Bharatiya Janata Party led central government and Uttar Pradesh state government when they started a new round of state reorganisation in 1998. Chosen for its allegedly less separatist connotations, the name change generated enormous controversy among many activists for a separate state who saw it as a political act. The name Uttarakhand remained popular in the region, even while Uttaranchal was promulgated through official usage.

In August 2006, Union Cabinet of India assented to the demands of the Uttaranchal Legislative Assembly and leading members of the Uttarakhand statehood movement to rename

Uttaranchal state as Uttarakhand. Legislation to that effect was passed by the Uttaranchal Legislative Assembly in October 2006, and the Union Cabinet brought in the bill in the winter session of Parliament. The bill was passed by Parliament and signed into law by then President A. P. J. Abdul Kalam in December 2006, and since January 1, 2007 the state has been known as Uttarakhand.

A BRIEF INTRODUCTION OF UTTARAKHAND

The 27th state of Republic of India, Devbhoomi Uttarakhand that was formed in the year 2000 after being separated from the large state of Uttar Pradesh, is a destination to explore the riches of Indian culture, history, and natural beauty. The state that borders Tibet to the north; Nepal to the east; the state of Uttar Pradesh to the south; and Himachal Pradesh to the west and north-west, is divided into regions, Garhwal and Kumaon, which further break into 13 districts. Earlier, the state was named Uttaranchal by Bhartiya Janta Party (BJP) led central government and Uttar Pradesh State Government when they started a fresh round of state reorganisation in 1998. However, in 2006, Union Cabinet of India to the agreed to the demands of the Uttaranchal Legislative Assembly and leading members of the Uttarakhand Statehood Movement and renamed Uttaranchal as Uttarakhand. The state also finds its mention in history as a part of the Kuru and the Panchal kingdoms (mahajanpads) during the Vedic age. In Hindu mythology also, Uttarakhand has been recognized as a part of the famed Kedarkhand (Now Garhwal) and Manaskhand (Kumaon). It is also believed the famous sage Vyas composed the epic of Mahabharata in Uttarakhand. The signs of the practise of Shaivism in ancient times along with Buddhism and Folk Shamanic religion was also found in the state.

Famed for their simple lifestyle, honesty, and humility, the people of Uttarakhand reflect a sincere bond with nature and gods. Although, the state has a fair amount of cities that are plush with all state-of-the-art amenities and crowd from other parts of the country, however, this could not take the people of

Uttarakhand away from their culture and traditional values. The culture of Uttarakhand still revolves around its traditional ethics, moral values, the simplicity of nature and a rich mythology.

People are divided into regions and are thus better recognized as Kumaoni (Inhabitants of Kumaon Region) and Garhwali (Inhabitants of Garhwal Region).

Apart from these two major inhabitants, Uttarakhand is also home to ethnic groups like Bhotias, Jaunsaries, Tharus, Bokshas, and Rajis. Although the major part of the region is seen speaking native languages like Kumaoni and Garhwali, Hindi, Urdu, and Punjabi are also widely spoken. Various tribal communities are both nomadic and those hailing from the Indo-Aryan descent are part of the ethnicity of Uttarakhand. Constituting of Proto-Australoid, Mongoloid, Nordic races and the Dravidians, the state is amongst one of the most historically affluent places in India. The ethnic groups like Jaunsari and Bhotias are further divided into small groups that corroborate the diverse population and culture in Uttarakhand.

The people of Uttarakhand indulge in vivid celebrations and performing of rituals around the year due to their deep-rooted collection with nature and the rich mythology. Like their simple lifestyle, the festivals and fairs in Uttarakhand are also simple yet culturally rich. Each season is welcome with hearty folk songs and dance and so are the agricultural periods. The ancestor spirit worship is exclusive to the state, Jaagar, as it is locally called, is held to wake the Gods and the local deities up from their inactive stage to solve their problems and shower on them many blessings. Dances like Barada Nati, Bhotiya Dance, Chancheri, Chhapeli, Choliya Dance, Jagars, Jhora, Langvir Dance, Langvir Nritya, Pandav Nritya, Ramola, Shotiya Tribal Folk Dances, Thali-Jadda, and Jhainta are performed on various occasions in Uttarakhand. The primary role of women is seen during the festivals as they are involved in preparing traditional dishes and singing folk songs. Dressed traditionally in Ghagra-Choli with a Rangwali (veil), these women look beautiful and their beauty is further enhanced by the big Nose Rings that are made of gold.

Truly, every day in Uttarakhand is a day of the festival; the noble and humble people take immense delight in celebrating even a small success with a grateful heart.

HISTORY OF UTTARAKHAND

Uttarakhand, India. Literally *Northern Land* or *Section* in Sanskrit, the name of Uttarakhand finds mention in the early Hindu scriptures as the combined region of Kedarkhand and Manaskhand.

Uttarakhand was the ancient Puranic term for the central stretch of the Indian Himalayas. Its peaks and valleys were well known in ancient times as the abode of gods and goddesses and source of the Ganges River. Today, it is often called "the Land of the Gods" (Devbhumi) because of the presence of a multitude of Hindu pilgrimage spots. Uttarakhand is known as Devbhumi from ancient times. The Pauravas, Kushanas, Kunindas, Guptas, Katyuris, Palas, the Chands, and Parmars or Panwars and the British have ruled Uttarakhand in turns.

History

The historical temples at Jageshwar, preserved by the Archaeological Survey of India

Ancient rock paintings, rock shelters, paleolithic stone tools (hundreds of thousands of years old), and megaliths provide evidence that the mountains of the region have been inhabited since prehistoric times. There are also archaeological remains which show the existence of early Vedic (c. 1500 BCE) practices in the area. The Pauravas, Kushanas, Kunindas, Guptas, Gurjara-Pratihara, Katyuris, Raikas, Palas, Chands, Parmars or Panwars, and the British have ruled Uttarakhand in turns.

The region was originally settled by Kol people, an aboriginal people of the Austro-Asiatic physical type who were later joined by the Indo-Aryan Khasas tribe that arrived from the northwest by the Vedic period (1700–1100 BCE). At that time, present-day Uttarakhand also served as a habitat for Rishis and Sadhus. It is believed that the sage Vyasa scripted the Hindu epic *Mahabharata* in the state. Among the first major dynasties of Garhwal and Kumaon were the Kunindas in the 2nd century BCE who practised an early form of Shaivism and traded salt with Western Tibet. It is evident from the Ashokan edict at Kalsi in Western Garhwal that Buddhism made inroads in this region. Folk shamanic practices deviating from Hindu orthodoxy also persisted here. However, Garhwal and Kumaon were restored to nominal Hindu rule due to the travails of Shankaracharya and the arrival of migrants from the plains.

Between the 4th and 14th centuries, the Katyuri dynasty dominated lands of varying extent from the Katyur (modern day Baijnath) valley in Kumaon. The historically significant temples at Jageshwar are believed to have been built by the Katyuris and later remodelled by the Chands. Other peoples of the Tibeto-Burman group known as Kirata are thought to have settled in the northern highlands as well as in pockets throughout the region, and are believed to be ancestors of the modern day Bhotiya, Raji, Buksa, and Tharu people.

By the medieval period, the region was consolidated under the Garhwal Kingdom in the west and the Kumaon Kingdom in the east. During this period, learning and new forms of painting (the Pahari school of art) developed. Modern-day Garhwal was likewise unified under the rule of Parmars who, along with many Brahmins and Rajputs, also arrived from the plains. In 1791, the expanding Gurkha Empire of Nepal overran Almora, the seat of the Kumaon Kingdom. It was annexed to Kingdom of Nepal by Amar Singh Thapa. In 1803, the Garhwal Kingdom also fell to the Gurkhas. After the Anglo-Nepalese War, this region was ceded to the British as part of the Treaty of Sugauli. The Garhwal Kingdom was then re-established from a smaller region in Tehri.

After India attained independence from the British, the Garhwal Kingdom was merged into the state of Uttar Pradesh, where Uttarakhand composed the Garhwal and Kumaon Divisions. Until 1998, Uttarakhand was the name most commonly used to refer to the region, as various political groups, including the Uttarakhand Kranti Dal (Uttarakhand Revolutionary Party), began agitating for separate statehood under its banner. Although the erstwhile hill kingdoms of Garhwal and Kumaon were traditional rivals the inseparable and complementary nature of their geography, economy, culture, language, and traditions created strong bonds between the two regions. These bonds formed the basis of the new political identity of Uttarakhand, which gained significant momentum in 1994, when demand for separate statehood achieved almost unanimous acceptance among both the local populace and national political parties.

The most notable incident during this period was the Rampur Tiraha firing case on the night of 1 October 1994, which led to a public uproar. On 24 September 1998, the Uttar Pradesh Legislative Assembly and Uttar Pradesh Legislative Council passed the Uttar Pradesh Reorganisation Bill, which began the process of creating a new state. Two years later the Parliament of India passed the Uttar Pradesh Reorganisation Act, 2000 and thus, on 9 November 2000, Uttarakhand became the 27th state of the Republic of India.

Uttarakhand is also well known for the mass agitation of the 1970s that led to the formation of the Chipko environmental movement and other social movements. Though primarily a livelihood movement rather than a forest conservation movement, it went on to become a rallying point for many future environmentalists, environmental protests, and movements the world over and created a precedent for non-violent protest. It stirred up the existing civil society in India, which began to address the issues of tribal and marginalized people. So much so that, a quarter of a century later, *India Today* mentioned the people behind the "forest satyagraha" of the Chipko movement as amongst "100 people who shaped India". One of Chipko's most salient features was the mass participation of female villagers. Both female and male activists played pivotal roles in the movement. Gaura Devi was the main activist who started this movement other participants were Chandi Prasad Bhatt, Sunderlal Bahuguna, and Ghanshyam Raturi, the popular Chipko poet.

MEANING OF NAME AND HISTORY

Uttarakhand is both the new and traditional name of the state that was formed from the hill districts of Uttar Pradesh, India. Uttarakhand is also the ancient Puranic term for the central stretch of the Indian Himalayas containing some of Hinduism's most sacred pilgrimage spots. Literally North Country or Section in Sanskrit, its peaks and valleys were well known in ancient times as the abode of gods and source of the Ganges River.

The region was dominated by the two kingdoms of Garhwal in the west and Kumaon in the east during the medieval period. In 1791, the expanding Gurkha Empire overran Almora, the seat of the Kumaon Kingdom. In 1803, the Garhwal Kingdom also fell to the Gurkhas. With the conclusion of the Anglo-Nepalese War in 1816, the Garhwal Kingdom was re-established from Tehri, and eastern British Garhwal and Kumaon retained as part of the Treaty of Sugauli.

In the post-independence period, the Tehri princely state was merged into Uttar Pradesh state, where Uttarakhand composed the Garhwal and Kumaon Divisions. Until 1998, Uttarakhand was the name most commonly used to refer to the region, as various political groups including most significantly the Uttarakhand Kranti Dal (Uttarakhand Revolutionary Party est. 1979), began agitating for separate statehood under its banner.

Although the erstwhile hill kingdoms of Garhwal and Kumaon were traditional rivals with diverse lingual and cultural influences due to the proximity of different neighbouring ethnic groups, the inseparable and complementary nature of their geography, economy, culture, language, and traditions created strong bonds between the two regions.

These bonds formed the basis of the new political identity of Uttarakhand, which gained significant momentum in 1994, when demand for its autonomy with India achieved almost unanimous acceptance among the people as well as the national political parties.

However, the term Uttarakhand came into use when the BJP-led central government initiated a new round of state reorganization in 2000 and imposed its preferred name. Chosen for its allegedly less separatist connotations, the name change generated enormous controversy among the rank and file of the separate state activists who saw it as a political act, however they were not quite as successful as Jharkhand state that successfully thwarted a similar move to impose the name Vananchal. Nevertheless, the name Uttarakhand remained popular in the region, even while Uttarakhand was promulgated and popularized through official usage.

In August 2006, India's Union Cabinet assented to the four-year-old demand of the Uttarakhand state assembly to rename Uttarakhand state as Uttarakhand. A legislation to that effect was passed by the State Legislative Assembly in October 2006, and the Union Cabinet brought in the bill in the winter session of Parliament. The bill was passed by Parliament and signed into law by the President in December 2006. Since then, Uttarakhand denotes a state in the Union of India.

Early history

The region was settled by the Kol people, a population speaking a language that belongs to the Munda language family. The Kol peoples were later joined by Indo-Aryan [Khas] tribes that arrived from the northwest by the Vedic period. At that time, present-day Uttarakhand also served as a haunt for Rishis and Sadhus. It is believed that Sage Vyasa scripted the Mahabharata here as the Pandavas are believed to have traveled and camped in the region. Among the first major dynasties of Garhwal and Kumaon were the Kunindas in the 2nd century B.C. who practiced an early form of Shaivism. They traded salt with Western Tibet. It is evident from the Ashokan edict at Kalsi, near Dehradun in Western Garhwal that Buddhism made inroads in this region. Shamanic religions are practiced by the Kol peoples and Folk Hinduism would emerge as a Hindu tradition distinct from Hindu orthodoxy. However, Garhwal and Kumaon were restored to nominal Brahmanical rule due to the travails of Shankaracharya and the arrival of migrants from the plains. In the fourth century, the Kunindas gave way to the Naga Dynasties. Between the 7th and 14th centuries, the Katyuri dynasty of Khas origin dominated lands of varying extent from the Katyur (modern day Baijnath) valley in Kumaon. Other peoples of the Tibeto-Burman group known as Kiratas are thought to have settled in the northern highlands as well as in pockets throughout the region, and believed to be the ancestors to the modern day Bhotiya, Raji, Buksha, and Tharu peoples.

By the medieval period, the region was consolidated under the Garhwal Kingdom in the west and the Kumaon Kingdom in the east. From the 13th–18th century, Kumaon prospered under the Chand Rajas who had their origins in the plains of India. During this period, learning and new forms of painting (the Pahari school of art) developed. Modern-day Garhwal was likewise unified under the rule of Parmar/Panwar Rajas, who along with a mass migration of Brahmins and Rajputs, also arrived from the plains. In 1791, the expanding Gurkha Empire of Nepal, overran Almora, the seat of the Kumaon Kingdom. In

1803, the Garhwal Kingdom also fell to the Gurkhas. With the conclusion of the Anglo-Nepalese War in 1816, a rump portion of the Garhwal Kingdom was reestablished from Tehri, and eastern *British* Garhwal and Kumaon ceded to the British as part of the Treaty of Sugauli.

Post-independence

In the post-independence period, the Tehri princely state was merged into Uttar Pradesh state, where Uttarakhand composed the Garhwal and Kumaon Divisions. Until 1998, Uttarakhand was the name most commonly used to refer to the region, as various political groups including most significantly the Uttarakhand Kranti Dal (Uttarakhand Revolutionary Party est. 1979), began agitating for separate statehood under its banner. Although the erstwhile hill kingdoms of Garhwal and Kumaon were traditional rivals with diverse lingual and cultural influences due to the proximity of different neighbouring ethnic groups, the inseparable and complementary nature of their geography, economy, culture, language, and traditions created strong bonds between the two regions. These bonds formed the basis of the new political identity of Uttarakhand, which gained significant momentum in 1994, when demand for separate statehood (within the Union of India) achieved almost unanimous acceptance among the local populace as well as political parties at the national level. Most notable incident during this period was the Rampur Tiraha firing case on the night of 1 October 1994, which led to public uproar and eventually to the division of the state of Uttar Pradesh in 2000.

However, the term *Uttaranchal* came into use when the Bharatiya Janata Party (BJP) led central and Uttar Pradesh state governments initiated a new round of state reorganization in 1998 and introduced its preferred name. Chosen for its allegedly less separatist connotations, the name change generated enormous controversy among the rank and file of the separate state activists who saw it as a political act, however they were not quite as successful as Jharkhand state that successfully thwarted a similar move to impose the name

Vananchal. Nevertheless, the name Uttarakhand remained popular in the region, even while Uttaranchal was promulgated through official usage.

In August 2006, India's Union Cabinet assented to the four-year-old demand of the Uttaranchal state assembly and leading members of the Uttarakhand movement to rename Uttaranchal state as Uttarakhand. Legislation to that effect was passed by the State Legislative Assembly in October 2006, and the Union Cabinet brought in the bill in the winter session of Parliament. The bill was passed by Parliament and signed into law by the President in December 2006. Since then, Uttarakhand denotes a state in India.

UTTARAKHAND MOVEMENT

Uttarakhand movement is termed to the events of statehood activism within the state Uttar Pradesh which ultimately resulted in a separate state Uttarakhand of the Republic of India. Uttarakhand became a separate state off Uttar Pradesh at 9 November 2000. It is notable that the formation of Uttarakhand was achieved with a very long struggle and heavy sacrifices. The first demand of Uttarakhand arose in 1897 and there had gradually been rising demand for a separate state several times. In 1994, the demand for statehood eventually took the form of mass movement that resulted in the forming of the country's 27th state by 2000.

Brief history

The important dates and events that played a key role in the struggle for the formation of the Uttarakhand state are:

- As a unit of Indian independence movement in 1913, national general convention of the Indian National Congress was held in Uttarakhand. Most representatives from Uttarakhand participated in the session. The same year in Uttarakhand, Tamta Sudharini Sabha held the convention for the upliftment of backwards and oppressed people of the area, as the *Shilpkar Mahasabha.*

- In September 1916, the Kumaon Parishad was founded by some young enthusiasts named mainly by Pt Hargovind vallabh Pant , Govind Ballabh Pant, Badri Datt Pandey, Indralal Shah, Mohan Singh Damarwal Chandra Lal Shah Prem Ballabh Pandey, Bhola Datt Pandey and Lakshmi Datt Shastri with the main objective to solve social and economic problems of the hill region. By 1916, in addition to the local general reforms, certain political objectives were added to the organization's goals. In the Provincial elections of 1923 and 1926 the candidates of Kumaon Parishad, Hargovind vallabh PantGovind Vallabh Pant , Mukundi Lal and Badri Datt Pandey badly defeated their counterparties.
- In 1926 Kumaon Parishad was merged in the Indian National Congress.
- In May 1938, according to official sources in then British Raj, in the national general convention of Indian National Congress held at Srinagar, Garhwal, Pandit Jawaharlal Nehrufavoured the cause of movement of the residents of hill region to have their own decisions according to their circumstances and supported the movement to enrich their culture.
- In 1940, at Haldwani conference, Badri Datt Pandey voiced for the special status of the mountainous region. Anusuya Prasad Bahuguna proposed the formation of Kumaon - Garhwal as the separate units. In 1954 the Uttar Pradesh Legislative Council member Indra Singh Nayal demanded the separate development plan for the highlands to then Chief Minister of Uttar Pradesh, Govind Ballabh Pant. In 1955 the Justice Fazal Ali commission recommended the Government of India, formation of hill region as a separate state.
- In the year 1957, deputy chairman of the Planning Commission, T. T. Krishnamachari suggested special attention to be given to the issues of hill region. In 12 May

1970, then Prime Minister Indira Gandhi addressed the issues of hill region and admitted that the diagnosis of the problems of hill region is the responsibility of both State and Central Governments. In 24 July 1979 the Uttarakhand Kranti Dal was founded in Mussoorie with the objective of the formation of a separate hill state. In June 1987 at the party convention of UKD in Karnaprayag, party leaders called for the constitution of conflict and isolation. In November 1987 UKD passed the party resolution for the formation of new state in the memorandum and the party president also sought to include Haridwar in the proposed state.

- Throughout the year 1994, students all over the region participated in the collective movement for separate statehood and reservations. Uttarakhand movement then further intensified in the field by Anti-Uttarakhand statement of then Chief Minister of Uttar Pradesh, Mulayam Singh Yadav. The leaders of UKD held fast-unto-death in the support of their demand for a separate state. State government employees struck work for three months, and the events of Uttarakhand movement got more inestisfied with the blockades and confrontation with the police. Uttarakhand activists in Mussoorie and Khatima were shot down by the police. Under the aegis of the *Samyukta Morcha* in 2 October 1994 the massive demonstrations and protests for the support of statehood took place in the national capital Delhi. Thousands of the Uttarakhand activists marched to the Delhi to take participation in this struggle. The activists peacefully taking part in the demonstration near Rampur Tiraha crossing, Muzaffarnagar were tortured and openly fired without any warning prior to the firing. Policemen were also alleged for indecent behavior and rapes with women activists.Satya Pokhriyal was leader who leads all the people from the misshappening, other andolankari help other people and shows the bravery. Several people were killed and many were injured. This misadventure by the police added fuel to the fire for Uttarakhand movement. The next day 3 October, the protests were called off for the demolition of firing and several deaths all over the region.

- 7 October 1994, a female activist died after the brutal attack by police in Dehradun while she was protesting against Rampur Tiraha Firings, and the activists in return stormed the police station.
- 15 October, curfew took in Dehradun and one activist was killed on the same day.
- 27 October 1994, then Home Minister of India, Rajesh Pilot held the talks with the statehood activists. Meanwhile, at Sriyantra Tapu, Srinagar several activists were killed in a brutal attack by the police.
- 15 August 1996, then Prime Minister H. D. Deve Gowda announced the formation of new state *Uttaranchal* from the Red Fort, Delhi.
- in 1998 the BJP-led coalition government in the center sent the 'Uttaranchal Bill' to the Government of Uttar Pradesh through the President of India. With 26 amendments the Uttaranchal Bill was passed by the Uttar Pradesh Assembly and sent back to the Central Government. The Central Government on 27 July 2000, presented the Uttar Pradesh Reorganisation Bill 2000 in the Parliament of India. It was passed by Lok Sabha on 1 August 2000, and the Rajya Sabha passed the bill on 10 August 2000. Then President of India, K. R. Narayanan approved the Uttar Pradesh Reorganisation Bill, on 28 August 2000, and then it turned into Act and on 9 November 2000 the new state Uttaranchal came into existence as the 27th state of India now known as Uttarakhand.

Events of the movement

There were several violent incidents in the state of Uttarakhand movement which are:

Khatima firing case

1 September 1994 is considered the darkest day of the Uttarakhand movement, such as police brutality since the day before the operation was not to look elsewhere. Indiscriminate firing by the police without warning the activists were up, resulting the death of seven activists.

Fallen Martyrs of the Khatima firing case:

- Martyr Late Bhagwan Singh, Village Sripur Bichhuwa, Khatima
- Martyr Late Dharmanand Bhatt, Village Amar Kalan, Khatima
- Martyr Late Gopichand, Village Ratanpur Phulaiya, Khatima
- Martyr Late Paramjit Singh, Rajivnagar, Khatima
- Martyr Late Pratap Singh, Khatima
- Martyr Late Rampal, Bareilly
- Martyr Late Salim Ahmad, Khatima

Bichpuri resident Mr. Bahadur Singh, Sripur Bichhuwa resident Mr. Puran Chand and Landour resident Mr. Rajendra Singh Panwar were also seriously injured in the police firing.

Mussoorie firing case

2 September 1994 Khatima firing silent march to protest police havoc once again broken out on people. The two real sisters to talk to the administration, the police shot at the office of activists in crèche. Indiscriminate firing by the police was to oppose it, which many people (about 21) was shot and died in the hospital of the three activists.

Fallen Martyrs of the Mussoorie firing case:

- Martyr Late Balbir Singh Negi (22), S/o Mr. Bhagwan Singh Negi, Lakshmi Misthanna Bhandar, Library, Mussoorie
- Martyr Late Belmati Chauhan (48), W/o Mr. Dharma Singh Chauhan, Village Khalon, Patti Ghat, Akodaya, Tehri

- Martyr Late Dhanpat Singh (50), Village Gangwara, Patti Gangwarsyun, Tehri
- Martyr Late Hansa Dhanai (45), W/o Mr. Bhagwan Singh Dhanai, Village Bangdhar, Patti Dharmadal, Tehri
- Martyr Late Madan Mohan Mamgain (45), Nagjali, Kulri, Mussoorie
- Martyr Late Rai Singh Bangari (54), Village Lavadi, Tilvada, Rudraprayag.

Rampur Tiraha (Muzaffarnagar) firing case

Going on the night of 2 October 1994 in Delhi rally Rampur Three way of activists, police authorities as repressed in Muzaffarnagar, the instance of any democratic country in the world so far not given any dictator that the unarmed activists night showered bullets were besieged in the dark around the mountain to the plain was abused women. The firing of the state were killed 7 activist. The tablet case, eight policemen guilty address, including three Inspahctor are being prosecuted on.

Fallen Martyrs of the Rampur Tiraha firing case:

- Martyr Late Ashok Kumar Kaishiv S/o Mr. Shiv Prasad Kaishiv Mandir Marg, Ukhimath, Rudraprayag
- Martyr Late Girish Bhadri (21), S/o Mr. Vachaspati Bhadri, Ajabpur Khurd, Dehradun
- Martyr Late Rajesh Lakhera (24), S/o Mr. Darshan Singh Lakhera, Ajabpur Kalan, Dehradun
- Martyr Late Rajesh Negi (20), S/o of Mr. Mahavir Singh Negi, Bhaniyawala, Dehradun
- Martyr Late Ravindra Singh Rawat (22), son of Mr. Kundan Singh Rawat, B-20, Nehru Colony, Dehradun
- Martyr Late Satendra Chauhan (16), S/o of Mr. Jodh Singh Chauhan, Village Haripur, Selaquin, Dehradun
- Martyr Late Suryaprakash Thapliyal (20), S/o Mr. Chintamani Thapliyal, Chaudah Bigha, Muni Ki Reti, Rishikesh

Dehradun firing case

3 October 1994 in Muzaffarnagar reach Dehradun reported case, people were bound to be fierce. Meanwhile, in this case, Martyr Late Ravindra Rawat situation after the funeral and fierce battles with the police and protesters in the entire Dehradun, which is already prepared to suppress the uprising in any condition The police firing, which has killed three people in the movement.

Fallen Martyrs of the Dehradun firing case:

- Martyr Late Balwant Singh Negi (45), S/o Mr. Bhagwan Singh Negi, Village Malhan, Nayagaon, Dehradun
- Martyr Late Deepak Walia (27), son of Mr. Om Prakash Walia, Village Badripur, Dehradun
- Martyr Late Rajesh Rawat (19), S/o Mrs. Anandi Devi, 27-Chandra Road, Nehru Colony, Dehradun

Late Rajesh Rawat's death was caused by the firing from the house of then Samajwadi Party leader Suryakant Dhasmana.

Kotdwar case

3 October 1994 meeting was boiled in protest scandal Uttarakhand Muzaffarnagar police administration was ready to suppress any kind of them. This link is also movement in Kotdwar, containing two activists by the police beating of rifle killed Bton and poles.

Fallen Martyrs of the Kotdwar case:

- Martyr Late Prithvi Singh Bisht, Manpur Khurd, Kotdwar
- Martyr Late Rakesh Devrani

Nainital firing case

At the opposite extreme in Nainital, but in the hands of intellectuals led by the police could not do anything, but he took it out over the Pacific Pratap Singh, who works at the hotel. Ar0a0f0 soldiers drawn from the hotel to avoid when it ran on Meghdoot Hotel, then was shot dead in his neck.

Fallen Martyrs of the Nainital firing case:

- Martyr Late Pratap Singh

Sriyantra Tapu (Srinagar) case

Srinagar town situated 2 km Sriyantra Tapu activists on 7 November 1994, against all repressive and isolated incidents Uttarakhand for the fast unto death started. 10 November 1994 the police climb to the island caused a havoc, many people have serious injuries, police said two men in order rifles from the dead butt and sticks-poles Alaknanda River was thrown in and the rain of stones, two of which died.

There bodies were not recovered by police till 15 days and Government bodies did not make any attempt to find the bodies, This information got spread and reached out to chairman of ex serviceman group (Virendra Prasad Kukshal), when he heard about the incident he sat for " Amaran Anshan" for 7 days, due to this Government bodies started the search and recovered the bodies. On 14 November 1994 deadbodies of the two martyrs were found floating in the Alaknanda river near Bagwan.

SPORTS

The high mountains and rivers of Uttarakhand attract many tourists and adventure seekers. It is also a favorite destination for adventure sports, such as paragliding, sky diving, rafting and bungee jumping.

More recently, golf has also become popular with Ranikhet being a favorite destination.

The Uttarakhand Cricket Association is the governing body for cricket activities and the Uttarakhand Cricket Team.

The Uttarakhand Football Association is the governing body for Association Football. The Uttarakhand football team represents Uttarakhand in the Santosh Trophy and other leagues.

2

Culture and Society

CULTURE

Uttarakhand's diverse ethnicities have created a rich literary tradition in languages including Hindi, Garhwali, Kumaoni, Jaunsari, and Bhoti. Many of its traditional tales originated in the form of lyrical ballads and chanted by itinerant singers and are now considered classics of Hindi literature.

Abodh Bandhu Bahuguna, Badri Datt Pandey, Ganga Prasad Vimal, Harikrishna Raturi, Mohan Upreti, Naima Khan Upreti, Prasoon Joshi, Shailesh Matiyani, Shekhar Joshi, Shivani, Shiv Prasad Dabral 'Charan', Taradutt Gairola, Tom Alter; Lalit Kala Akademi fellow — Ranbir Singh Bisht; Sangeet Natak Akademi awardees — B. M. Shah, Prem Matiyani and Urmil Kumar Thapliyal; Sahitya Akademi awardees — Leeladhar Jagudi, Manglesh Dabral, Manohar Shyam Joshi, Ramesh Chandra Shah, Ruskin Bond and Viren Dangwal; Jnanpith Awardee and Sahitya Akademi fellow Sumitranandan Pant are some major literary, artistic and theatre personalities from the state.

Prominent philosophers and environmental activists Gaura Devi, Chandi Prasad Bhatt, Sunderlal Bahuguna and Vandana Shiva are also from Uttarakhand.

The dances of the region are connected to life and human existence and exhibit myriad human emotions. Langvir Nritya is a dance form for males that resembles gymnastic movements. Barada Nati folk dance is another dance of Jaunsar-Bawar, which is practised during some religious festivals. Other well-known dances include Hurka Baul, Jhora-Chanchri, Chhapeli, Thadya, Jhumaila, Pandav, Chauphula, and Chholiya.

Sumitranandan Pant Museum, Kausani

Music is an integral part of the Uttarakhandi culture. Popular types of folk songs include Mangal, Basanti, Khuder and Chhopati. These folk songs are played on instruments including dhol, damau, turri, ransingha, dholki, daur, thali, bhankora, mandan and mashakbaja. "Bedu Pako Baro Masa" is a popular folk song of Uttarakhand with international fame and legendary status within the state. It serves as the cultural anthem of Uttarakhandi people worldwide. Music is also used as a medium through which the gods are invoked. *Jagar* is a form of spirit worship in which the singer, or *Jagariya*, sings a ballad of the gods, with allusions to great epics, like Mahabharat and Ramayana, that describe the adventures and exploits of the god being invoked. Basanti Devi Bisht, Chander

Singh 'Rahi', Gopal Babu Goswami, Heera Singh Rana, Narendra Singh Negi and Meena Rana are popular folk singers and musicians from the state, so is country music singer Bobby Cash.

Architectural details of a Dharmashala, established 1822, Haridwar

Among the prominent local crafts is wood carving, which appears most frequently in the ornately decorated temples of Uttarakhand.

Intricately carved designs of floral patterns, deities, and geometrical motifs also decorate the doors, windows, ceilings, and walls of village houses. Paintings and murals are used to decorate both homes and temples.

Pahari painting is a form of painting that flourished in the region between the 17th and 19th century. Mola Ram started the Garhwal Branch of the Kangra school of painting. Guler State was known as the "cradle of Kangra paintings". Kumaoni art often is geometrical in nature, while Garhwali art is known for its closeness to nature. Other crafts of Uttarakhand include handcrafted gold jewellery, basketry from Garhwal, woollen shawls, scarves, and rugs. The latter are mainly produced by the Bhotiyas of northern Uttarakhand.

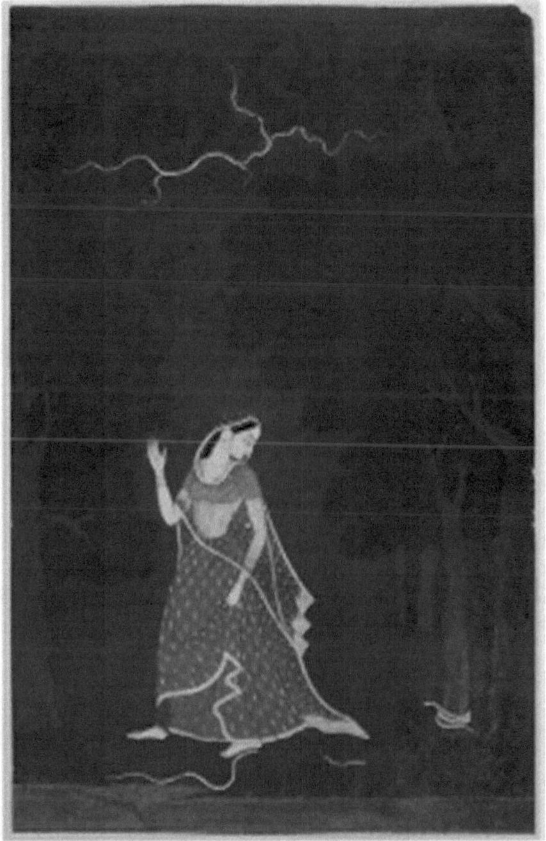

Abhisarika Nayika, *a painting by Mola Ram*

The primary food of Uttarakhand is vegetables with wheat being a staple, although non-vegetarian food is also served. A distinctive characteristic of Uttarakhand cuisine is the sparing use of tomatoes, milk, and milk based products. Coarse grain with high fibre content is very common in Uttarakhand due to the harsh terrain. Crops most commonly associated with Uttarakhand are Buckwheat (locally called *Kotu* or *Kuttu*) and the regional crops, *Maduwa* and *Jhangora*, particularly in the interior regions of Kumaon and Garhwal. Generally, either Desi Ghee or Mustard oil is used for the purpose of cooking food.

Simple recipes are made interesting with the use of hash seeds *Jakhiya* as spice. Bal Mithai is a popular fudge-like sweet. Other popular dishes include Dubuk, Chains, Kap, Bhatiya, Phana, Paliyo, Chutkani and Sei. In sweets; Swal, Ghughut/Khajur, Arsa, Mishri, Gatta and Gulgulas are popular. A regional variation of Kadhi called *Jhoi* or *Jholi* is also popular.

Bathing ghat on the Ganges during Kumbh Mela, 2010, Haridwar

One of the major Hindu pilgrimages, Haridwar Kumbh Mela, takes place in Uttarakhand. Haridwaris one of the four places in India where this mela is organised. Haridwar most recently hosted the Purna Kumbh Mela from Makar Sankranti (14 January 2010) to Vaishakh Purnima Snan (28 April 2010). Hundreds of foreigners joined Indian pilgrims in the festival which is considered the largest religious gathering in the world. Kumauni Holi, in forms including Baithki Holi, Khari Holi and Mahila Holi, all of which start from Vasant Panchami, are festivals and musical affairs that can last almost a month. Ganga Dashahara, Vasant Panchami, Makar Sankranti, Ghee Sankrant, Khatarua, Vat Savitri, and Phul Dei are other major festivals. In addition, various fairs like Kanwar Yatra, Kandali Festival, Ramman, Harela Mela, Kauthig, Nauchandi Mela, Giddi Mela, Uttarayani Mela and Nanda Devi Raj Jat Mela take place.

PEOPLE

The native people call themselves Garhwali/Kumaoni and more than 90% of them are Hindus. Many also colloquially call themselves Pahari meaning "hill person" to distinguish themselves from Desis of the rest of India. Most identify themselves as upper caste, however the scheduled caste section of the population preceded the later migrants in settling the hills. The upper castes can be further subdivided into two Indo-Aryan groups, the original Khas tribes that arrived in the hills by the Vedic era and later migrants from North-Central India that arrived in the medieval period. Admixture and caste mobility has reduced the distinction between the two groups, although some areas such as Jaunsar-Bawar are believed by anthropologists to represent the pure Khas group.

Other ethnic communities in the region include the Jadh, Marcha, Tolcha, and Shauka (Rung) of the Indo-Tibetan frontier, collectively known as the Bhotiya, the Buksha and Tharu tribal people of the southeastern Terai region, the Raji or Vanrawats of Askot in Pithoragarh district, and nomadic cattle herders known as Gujjar in the southwestern Terai. Many Punjabis arrived after the partition of India, and along with migrants from the adjoining plains, make up the majority of the Terai population. Nepalis, Bengalis, and Tibetans of Eastern Tibet region (Khampa) have also settled in the state.

Kumaoni and Garhwali dialects are spoken is Kumaon and Garhwal region respectively. Jaunsari and Bhotiya is also spoken in the region by some tribal communities. In various regions a mixture of both Kumaoni and Garhwali is also spoken. The city population however converse mostly in Hindi. The majority of people in this state are Rajputs.

Social Groups

Bhotiya: The Bhotiya are a people living in the trans-Himalayan region that divides India from Tibet. They are closely related to the Tibetans and their name, Bhotiya, derives from the word Bod, which is the Classical Tibetan name for

Tibet. Those living in Uttarakhand are generally referred to as Bhotiya, although they are sometimes also referred to as Bhutia; Bhutia more commonly means the related people of Sikkim.

The Indian government uses the word Bhotiya to refer to those who have traditionally resided in the upper Himalayan valleys of the Kumaon and Garhwal of Uttarakhand Himalayas. These include the Shaukas of Kumaon and Tolchhas and Marchhas of Garhwal.

The Bhotiya speak languages belonging to the Tibeto-Burman family, although their dialects are mutually unintelligible to the Tibetans and Garwhalis. Owing to social process of Sanskritization, many of them have intermarried with the Hindus over the years.

Most of the Bhotiya practice a combination of Tibetan Buddhism, Bon and Hinduism, although Hinduism is prevalent among the earlier semi-Indian groups, while Buddhism is prevalent among the recent immigrant groups of purer Tibetan origin, such as the Jadh.

Hindu gods such as the weather God Gabla, Runiya and Suniya, are worshipped to protect their animals from disease. Sidhuwa and Bidhuwa are worshipped as well to find lost animals.

Ethnic Groups

Jadh: Inhabiting in the Uttarkashi region of Uttarakhand, most Jadh can be found in the villages of Nelang and Jadhang between Himachal Pradesh and Uttarakhand, who were both situated at an elevation of 3,400m in the Bhagirathi valley. These towns are only as near as thirty miles from the Tibetan border, and a small number have relocated to Harsil. Their language resembles closely to Tibetan.

Originally traders, the Jadh lead a semi-nomadic lifestyle and maintained social ties with the neighbouring Kinnauries, Jaunsaries and Tibetans. Until the closure of the Tibetan border in 1962, the Jadh barter-traded with the Tibetans across the high Himalayan paths, notably along traditional routes such as the Thang-La and Tang-Choke-La, which is situated at an elevation of 5,050 m and 5,400 m respectively. Basic items such as cotton, grains, metal, oil seeds and sugar are traded in various Tibetan markets across the border. In exchange, they received salt, wool and borax, which is sold by Tibetan traders in the towns of Uttarkashi and Bushahr. With the reopening of the border in the 1990's, trading activities have resumed to a lesser extent.

Today, the Jadh graze their sheep and goats in the Upper Jahnvi Valley during the warm summer months, when the alpine vegetation is in full bloom. Upon the coming of autumn, they move down to the lower hills, reaching the temperate forests bordering Rishikesh by October. As of today, each Jadh family could own as many as 200 to 400 animals, principally yak herds. The number of livestock owned by them is a measure of their wealth and economic condition.

The Jadh used to migrate from these high altitude villages in winter in the past with their entire families. In modern days, some families and a few shopkeepers have decided to stay back in Dunda, which is not far removed from their native homeland, while the rest of them move to the forests around Rishikesh. Upon the coming of spring, the Jadh will return to their homeland.

Most Jadh women wear their hair in a turban or a plait, owing to its cold weather. They wear a costume which resembles a cross between the Tibetan and Garwhali styles. The men, on the other hand, will wear the nomadic Tibetan clothing.

The Jadh are followers of Tibetan Buddhism and to a lesser extent, Bon, although minimal Hindu influence can be seen. Adhering to the caste system loosely, the Jadh classify themselves as Rajput. Buddhist Lamas are employed to conduct religious ceremonies and medical treatment.

Marcha: The Marcha live in the Mana and Niti valleys on the cold and dry tracts of Upper Chamoli, which is also known as the Painkhanda tract. Though they speak a Tibeto-Burman language, their facial features suggest some intermarriage with the Indians. Because they originally migrated from Tibet, the Marcha follow Hinduism. Unlike the other Bhotiya groups, they worship in Hindu temples, and rely on the Hindu Brahmins to conduct religious ceremonies. Doctors, known as Vaidyas, are employed to treat patients.

Traditionally, most Marcha were nomadic shepherds and herders. Typically the men work as shepherds rearing sheep and goats, while the women stay in the villages tending the fields. Crops grown in these high mountain areas include rajma (beans), aloo (potatoes), mutter (peas) as well as several different varieties of grains. These animals graze on the rich alpine pastures in the summer, and move to lower altitudes in the winter. The herders sell wool, meat, and milk to earn a living.

The Marcha long maintained links with the Tibetans by barter trading through the Mana and Niti passes, which are at an elevation of 5,800m. The Indo-Tibetan border was closed in 1962. Before it closed, large numbers of caravans of mules, yaks, and the hardiest men would travel into Tibet laden with Indian goods when the snow melted.

In trading centres, they bartered their goods for local Tibetan merchandise (e.g., wool and salt), to be resold in local markets in India. The merchants would return to Indian just before the start of the winter season in October. Since the Indo-Tibetan border was closed in 1962, the Marcha have taken to a semi-agrarian and semi-nomadic lifestyle. Limited trading links were reopened in 1992.

Rangkas: The isolated Rangkas tribe, whose population host a meagre 600, is found in the outskirts of the Mahakali valley. According to ethnologue, the Rangkas are ethnically related or are of the Johar tribe.

Shauka: Shaukas, further consist of several subgroups, residing in two different river valleys. Joharis live along the Goriganga river valley in Munsiyari Tehsil of Pithoragarh district, while the Rungs live along the Mahakali river valley in Dharchula tahsil and Darchula district of Nepal.

Byansi/Byangkhupa: The Byansis (called 'Byangkhupa' in

'Rung') are a subgroup of an ethnic group called Rung/Shaukas living along the upper valleys of Mahakali and its tributary Dhauliganga, high up in the Himalayas where Uttarakhand of India, Ali district of western Tibet and Darchula of Nepal meet. Byans (or 'Byangkhoin 'Rung') consists of seven villages (Kuti, Rongkang, Nabi, Gunji, Napalchyo, Garbyang, Budi) on the Indian side and two villages (Chhangru and Tinkar) on the Nepal side.

Their religion is a mixture of Bon, Hinduism, Buddhism and animism. Each clan, of which there are many in each village, has its own clan god(s). Ancestral worship ('simi thuma') is a very important part of Byansi religion. Their language falls under Tibeto-Burman group. Three distinct dialects are spoken in Byans region — Byangkhu lo, Kutpa lo and Tinkar lo.

Chaundasi/Bangbani: Chaundasis live in fourteen (chaudha) villages along the upper hilly area of Mahakali river between India and Nepal. Locally the area is known as Bangba and the residents Bangbani. Main villages include Ponggong, Rongto, Monggong, Soso, Sirdang, Shirkha, Rung and Tijya, which are between the altitude of 7000 and 9000 ft. Chaundasis speak a separate dialect of Shauka called 'Bangba lo'.

Darmiya/Darmani: The Darmanis live in the Darma valley of Dhauliganga, a tributary of Mahakali river. Along with the Byangkhupas and Bangbanis, they form the three subgroups of Rung. They speak 'Darma lo', which is markedly different from 'Byankho lo' or 'Banga lo', and is considered by many to be the original Rung language. Main villages include Sela, Chal, Soan, Seepu, Bon, Dugtu, Daatu, Nangling, Marchha, Bongling, Gow, Dakar, Filam, Tidang, Baling, Durr.

Johar: The Shauka living in the Johar valley of Goriganga river in Munsyari Tehsil of the Pithoragarh district are also known as Johari or Johari Shauka. They are one of the few Bhotiya tribes that shows a rich cultural heritage and adhere to the caste system. Shaukas are the followers of Hinduism, and rely on the Hindu Brahmins to conduct religious ceremonies. Their main deity is Goddess Nanda Devi in Martoli and Milam.

The legend of Rajuli - Malusahi relates to Rajuli, daughter of Sunpati Shauka (A local lord/king of Johar) and Malusahi, son of the Katyuri King of Bageshwar. The famous explorers Pundit Nain Singh Rawat (C.I.E.) and Rai Bahadur Kisan Singh Rawat belongs to the Johar valley.

Rung: The Shauka live in Chaudas, Vyas and Darma valleys and in Munsiyari in the Pithoragarh district in Kumaon, and as well as parts of extreme northwest Nepal. They are also known as Rang and speak a distinct Tibeto-Burman dialect, which is barely intelligible with Magar. According to legend, they are of Tibetan and Kiranti origin, although it seems that they are of solely of Tibetan origin.

The Shauka have their own scripts, which is now extinct. According to anthropologists, portions of it dating back to the 12th century can be found in the caves of the mountains.

Influenced by and practising Tibetan Buddhist, Bon and Hindu religions together, the Shauka are one of the few Bhotiya tribes that shows a rich cultural heritage and adhere to the caste system. Like the Jadh, the Shauka rely on Lamas to conduct ceremonies and rituals in the Buddhist Gompas and celebrate Tibetan festivals such as Losar, and Hindu and Animist gods such as Gabladev in Darma, Chaudans and Byans. Another Bon deity, especially in Rolpa, Ramjung is also worshipped. Buddhist prayer flags, locally known as Dharchyo, is hung outside houses.

The dress of the Shauka is known as Chyungbala, which reflects little Tibetan or local influences, but their skills in weaving, spinning and natural dyeing. Major festivals such as Dhhyoula and Kangdali are celebrated, although minor festivals such as Kangdali, Syangthangapujan, Syeemithhumo (atma pujan), Maati (Soil) pooja, and Nabu Samo and the annual Kanda-Utsav are also celebrated. Another fair which celebrates the success of their trade, the Jauljibi and Thal is celebrated, because the Shauka are also reported to have conducted trade between Taklakot in Tibet and Darchula, and to a lesser extent, the Tharu people in the Terai.

The legend of the Kandali Festival comes a folklore, which tells of a boy who died upon applying the paste of the root from a shrub known as Kang-Dali on his boil. Enraged, his widowed mother cursed the shrub and ordered the Shauka women to pull up the root of the Kang-Dali plant off its ground upon reaching its full bloom, which happens once in twelve years. According to another story, the Kangdali festival is to commemorate the brave women who repelled the enemy while their husbands were away. Hiding in the Kandali bushes, they attacked the bushes, which subsequently destroyed the enemy.

Since then, a victory dance is performed every twelve years upon the decimation this shrub in its blooming period. The women with lead the procession, each armed with a ril, a tool which was used in compacting carpet on the loom. The children and men armed with swords and shields would follow closely behind. As they sing and dance, their music echoes in the valley, and upon approaching the blooms, warlike tunes are played and war cries are uttered. The women, fierce as they were, attacked the bushes with their rils. The menfolk will follow up and the bushes are hacked with swords, who will uproot the bushes and take them back, as the spoils of the war. In turn, victory cries are raised and rice grains are again cast towards the sky to honour the deities with the prayer that the people of Chaundas Valley may be ever victorious over enemies. After the victory dance and the extermination of the shrub, the festival is concluded with a feast.

Tolcha: A small Bhotiya tribe living in the Niti valley among the Marcha tribe, the Tolcha, like the Marcha, are Hindu. Despite the fact that they are of Tibetan origin, Indian intermarriage over the centuries have made the Tolcha tribe resembling much more closely to the Indian Jaunsari than the Tibetans.

Pokhariya: Pokhariya or Pokharia is the group of people live in the newly formed state of Uttarakhand, India. It is an old Rajput clan living in the Garkha region of Pithoragarh district in the Kanalichhina developmental block of Didihat Tehsil. The history of Pokhariya's Rajput clan traces back to the medieval period. They were primarily from the area now called Pokharan in modern Rajesthan. Muslim attackers attempted to convert them there; seeking to preserve their purity of blood, they refused to submit and waged guerilla warfare against the Muslims. They later moved to Nepal and settled near modern Pokhara in Nepal. They conflicted with natives there, and later on moved and settled in the present place in Uttarakhand. The clan has a number of traditions such as Jatta, Anthoo, Harela and prayer and Gandeli to deities such as Hushkar', Balchhin ,'Kalua and Kalchhin and Garh-Devi (deity of fort). Pokhariya are confined to Dangti, Dungara and Dokuna.

KUMAONI CULTURE

Kumaon: The culture of the present Kumaon is a blend of influences from the indigenous population as well as from the immigrants to this region. Consequently, the myths, dialects, languages, folk literature, festivals, fairs and forms of artistic expression are examples of the creative influences of the different cultural groups that constitute Kumaon.

Every peak, lake or mountain range is somehow or the other connected with some myth or the name of a God or Goddess, ranging from those associated with the Shiva, Shakta and Vaishnava traditions, to local Gods like Ham, Saim, Golla, Chhurmal, Kail Bisht, Bholanath, Gangnath, Airy and Chaumu. Temples are dedicated to the nine famous Goddesses, other local Goddesses, Bhairava, Surya:. and Ganesh. The temples at Jageshwar, Bageshwar, Binsar, Thalkedar, Rameshwar, Pancheshwar, Baijnath and Gananath are devoted to Lord Shiva. The temples of Devidhura, Gangolihat, Pumagiri, Almora, Nainital, Kot Ki Mai and Kotgari Devi are associated with the Shakt tradition, while the region of Lohaghat - Champawat (Mount Kandeo) is associated with Kunna Avatar. This region also has two famous Sun temples.

According to Atkinson there were 35 Vaishnava and 250

Shiva temples in British Kumaon. Eight Vaishnava and 64 Shiva temples were dedicated to the Shakti or female form alone.

Although Lord Shiva's influence prevailed throughout Kumaon, mainly because of its proximity to the region of Panchkedars and Kailash - Mansarovar, this did not in any way hamper the influence of the local folk Gods and Goddesses. Although the tales of Nanda Devi and Naina Devi have now been linked together, they began as two different stories.

FOLK GODS OF KUMAON

In spite of being worshippers of Lord Shiva and Shakti, the people of Kumaon have a rich tradition of folk deity worship. The heroes of some long - forgotten age have later on become folk gods and they give expression to the popular beliefs of the people. Each folk god has a separate story attached to his name and each one is remembered through some peak, temple or jagar (a form of ritual folk poem). It is believed that Kumaon once had a tradition of Yaksha worship. The presence of 'Naga' or snake worship is an indication of the reverence' given to the brave. Besides worshipping the usual gods and goddesses associated with Hinduism, the people of Kumaon have also worshipped Kul Devatas (family gods), Gram Devatas (village gods), Naga Devatas (snake gods), Bhumi Devatas (land gods) and Veers (the brave heroes). The following are the important folk gods & goddesses of Kumaon:

Naina Devi: Naina Devi is a name for the Goddess Parvati. According to the Jagars Naina Devi was established in Kumaon by the Katyuri queen Jiya Rani. On the other hand there is a myth which talks of Sati's committing suicide by jumping into a sacrificial fire, when she and Lord Shiva were insulted by her father Dakshaprajapati during a Yajnya, to which Shiva and Sati had not been invited in the first place. The myth goes on to say that while Shiva was taking Sati's body away, her eye fell down at a spot near the temple of Pashan Devi in Nainital. Therefore, according to myth Naina Devi is none other than the goddess Parvati. (It is the story that Sati was reborn as Parvati).

Nanda Devi: Nanda Devi is the Greek Goddess 'Nana', who came to the Himalaya with the Indo - Greeks and Kushan Kings. However, the fact remains that Nanda Devi is typically a Kumaoni goddess and most popular in the region. Referring to the rich religious myths and lores associated with Uttarakhand, E.T.Atkinson has said: 'To the beliefs of the great majority of Hindus, the Kumaon (Himalaya) is what Palestine is to the Christian.'

Bholanath: Bholanath is the most popular and revered folk god of Kumaon. He is said to be an incarnation of Lord Shiva. According to legend, the Chand King, Udai Chand, disinherited his elder son because of his bad habits and gave the Kingdom to his younger son. After wandering for a long time the elder son came with his pregnant wife and settled down near Almora. The King had both of them executed. The son, his wife and their unborn child became ghosts and people started worshipping them. The original temple of Bholanath is at Champawat.

Gwalla: Gwalla is also called Gorilla or Golla or Golu. Banners and flags are hung up over many temples in honour of Gwalla. There are Gwalla temples at Champawat, Chitai and Ghorakhal, although the temple at Chitai is the most famous of them. The story about Gwalla talks of a local king who, while hunting, sent his servants to look for water. The servants disturbed a woman who was praying.

The woman, in a fit of anger, taunted the king that he could not separate two fighting bulls and proceeded to do so herself. The king was very impressed by this deed and he married the lady. When this queen got a son, the other queens, who were jealous of her, placed a pumpkin in its place and the child in a cage and put the cage into the river. The child was brought up by a fisherman. When the boy grew up he took a wooden horse to the river and on being questioned by the queens he replied that if women can give birth to pumpkins then wooden horses can drink water. When the king heard about this, he punished the guilty queens and crowned the boy, who went on to be known as Gwalla devata.

Gangnath: Gangnath's story is like the story of Bholanath. Gangnath was the son of king Vaibhav Chand of Doti (Western Nepal). He fought with his father and left his house when he fell in love with a Joshi Brahmin lady Bhana. Bhana's father/husband got Gangnath murdered by a blacksmith. When Gangnath took to harming people, they started worshipping him and Bhana. The jagar singers of Kumaon often tell tales about the love affair of Gangnath and Bhana. Gangnath temples are spread all over Kumaon.

Airy: Airy, whose eyes are said to be on the top of his head, is worshipped like the God Shani. His attendants, "Sau" and "Bhau" ride on dogs. Airy is said to take care of animals and it is in this form that he is worshipped. There are numerous temples of Airy in Kumaon but the main temple is at Byandhura.

Kail Bisht: Kail Bisht is said to be a generous folk god. The temple of this flute playing God is near Binsar. The story goes that Shrikrishna Pandey was given false reports about a love affair between his wife and a brave Rajput shepherd Kallu (Kail Bisht). The matter was brought before the king, who refused to have Kail Bisht executed when he saw the impression of a trident on Kail Bisht's forehead and that of a Kadamb flower on his feet. However, later on Kallu was murdered by deception.

Chaumu: This god is worshipped as a protector of animals particularly in the Jhulaghat-Pancheswar region. There is a story about a man who was going to Champawat with a Shivlinga in his turban. When he stopped to drink water he placed his turban on the road, but he could not pick it up again. Later on people started worshipping this spot. Bells and milk are offered in the temples of Chaumu at Chaupakhia (Wadda, Pithoragarh), Chamdeval (Pulla, Champawat), Pancheswar, Thathgaon (Almora), Dhamkuri, Surar and Santola (all in Nepal). These are basically the seats of seven brothers. Chamdeval is the principal seat of Chaumu.

Haru: Harish Chandra was a famous king of Champawat, who after his death was worshipped as the folk god Haru. Haru's mother's name was Kainar and he is said to be Gwall's maternal uncle. The temples of Haru and Saim, the god of boundaries, are generally together.

Besides these, many other folk gods are worshipped in Kumaon e.g. Bhumia, Balchan, Nagnath, Bhandari Golla, Badhan, Narsingh, Lataul, Gabla, Chhurmal etc. Anyari and Ujyali are the popular goddesses. Garh Devis are to be found in cremation grounds and are worshipped on the night of Amavasya. Although Bafaul, Ramol, Sangram Karki are also mentioned as folk heroes, they are not treated like gods.

KUMAUNI PEOPLE

Kumauni or Kumaoni or Kumai(as said in Nepal) are people from Kumaon region of Uttarakhand, India. In colloquial language, people of Kumaon are also referred to as "Pahari". Kumainis addressed to person having origin in Kumaon region. The word Kumain is a direct derivative of Kumaoni.

They include all those who speak the Kumaoni language or any of its numerous dialects, living in the Almora, Bageshwar, Champawat, Pithoragarh, Nainital, Dehradun, Udham Singh Nagar, districts of Uttarakhand, India and Doti, Khaptad, Bajang region of Nepal.

History

British Raj

The Kumaon Regiment, established at Ranikhet in 1917, still gets its recruits from the Kumaonis of the Kumaon division and the Ahir from the plains.

There were widespread opposition to British rule in various parts of Kumaon. The Kumauni people, especially the Champawat District, rose in rebellion against the British during the Indian Rebellion of 1857 under the leadership of Kalu Singh Mahara.

Language

UNESCO designated Kumaoni as language in the *unsafe* category which requires consistent conservation efforts.

Culture

Festivals

After harvesting season people mostly relax, rejoice, dance and sing, and thus a festival is generated. At the transition of the sun from one constellation to another Sankranti is observed. Each Sankranti has a fair or festival connected to it somewhere in Kumaon. Fooldeyi, Bikhauti, Harela, Ghee Sankranti, Khatarua, Uttaraini and Ghughutiya are the most-observed Sankranties throughout the region. Other festivals have the bearings in the moon and thus the dates change frequently in the Gregorian Calendar. Basant Panchami, Shiv Ratri, Holi, Samvatsar Parwa, Ram Navami, Dashra, Batsavitri, Rakshabandhan, Janmastmi, Nandastmi, and Deepawali are some of the auspicious occasions.

Dasshera or Bijaydashmi

Dasshera festival starts in Kumaon with the performance of *Ramlila*, which is itself unique as it is based on the musical rendering of the *katha* or story of Lord Ram based on the theatrical traditions set by Uday Shankar while on his stay in Almora. These traditions were further enriched by Mohan Upreti and Brijendra Lal Sah. Known as the Almora or Kumaon style, Ramlila has been recognised by UNESCO as one of the representative styles of Ramlila in India.

Theatre

Kumaoni theatre, which developed through its 'Ramleela' plays, later evolved into a modern theatre form through the efforts of theatre stalwarts like Mohan Upreti and Dinesh Pandey and groups like 'Parvatiya Kala Kendra' (started by Mohan Upreti) and 'Parvatiya Lok Kala Manch'. Besides this the famous Hindi poet, Sumitranandan Pant also hailed from Kausani, district Bageshwar.

Radio

- Trans World Radio (USA) – 7320 Hz (Shortwave)

Cuisine

Kumaoni food is simple and comprises largely of vegetables and pulses. It is highly nutritious to enable survival in the hard environment of the hills and cold climate.

Vegetables like potato (*aaloo*), radish (*mooli*), colocacia leaves (*arbi ke patte, papad*), pumpkin (*kaddoo*), spinach (*palak*) and many others are grown locally by the largely agrarian populace and consumed in various forms.

List of Kumaoni/Kumai people

- Bharat Ratna Govind Ballabh Pant, Union Home Minister (10 January 1955 – 7 March 1961), Chief Minister of Uttar Pradesh (26 January 1950 – 27 December 1954), Premier of United Provinces (17 July 1937 – 2 November 1939) and (1 April 1946 – 25 January 1950)
- B. D. Pande (ICS), Union Cabinet Secretary, Governor of Punjab, Governor of Bengal, Administrator of Chandigarh

GARHWALI PEOPLE

Garhwali people are an Indo-Aryan ethno-linguistic group who primarily live in the Garhwal Himalayas of the northernIndian state of Uttarakhand and speak the Indo-Aryan Garhwali language. Any person who has ancestral Garhwali roots or lives in Garhwal and has a Garhwali heritage is called a Garhwali.

They include all those who speak the Garhwali language or any of its numerous dialects, living in Dehradun, Haridwar, Tehri Garhwal, Pauri Garhwal, Uttarkashi, Chamoli and Rudraprayag districts of Uttarakhand, India.

Significant communities of Garhwali diaspora live in the Indian states of Uttar Pradesh, Himachal Pradesh, Haryana, Delhi, Punjab, Madhya Pradesh, Rajasthan and Maharashtra along with a sizable population overseas. According to various estimates, there are at least 2.5 million Garhwali migrants living in Delhi and the National Capital Region.

Etymology

In modern usage, "Garhwali" is used to refer to anyone whose linguistic, cultural, and ancestral or genetic origins are from the Garhwal Himalayas. Their ethnonym is derived from the word '*Garhwal*' or '*Gadwal*'. The exact origin of the word Garhwal is unknown, though it is believed to be derived from the title '*Garh-wala*' (owner of forts) given to the ruler Ajay Pal, who is said to have consolidated 52 principalities to form the kingdom in the 14 century. After this conquest the domain under Ajay Pal is said to have been called '*Garhwal*', possibly due to the numerous forts in the region.

The name of the region and its people prior to Ajay Pal is unknown though some historians like Atkinson have alluded to '*Khas-des*' (Land of the Khasas) and Sircar has stated that '*Stri-Rajya*' (Kingdom of Women) as the ancient name of Garhwal and Kumaon. However, we have no proof to corroborate these claims. The earliest reference to places in this region are in the Skanda Purana as '*Kedar Khand*' and in the Mahabharata as '*Himvat*' to describe the area that contained Gangadwar (Haridwar and Kankhala), Badrinath, Gandhamardan, and Kailash.

Garhwal Kingdom

The Kingdom of Garhwal was founded by Panwar Rajputs nearly 700 years ago at a place called Chandpur Garhi. Earlier Garhwal used to have 52 principalities called Garhs(cluster of habitations). Garh was ruled by a Chief, one of these chiefs, Ajai Pal ruler of Chandpur Garhi from Panwar dynasty, reduced all the minor principalities under his own sway with the power of his sword, and founded the Garhwal Kingdom. He and his descendants ruled over Garhwal in an uninterrupted line till 1803, when the Gurkhas invaded Kumaon and Garhwal, driving the Garhwal chief into the plains. For twelve years the Gurkhas ruled the country with a rod of iron, until a series of encroachments by them on British territory led to the Anglo–Nepalese War in 1814. At the termination of the campaign,

Garhwal Kingdom and Kumaon Kingdomwere converted into British districts, while the Tehri principality was restored to a son of deceased king Pradyumn Shah, King Sudarshan Shah. Another part taken by British was called British Garhwal and had an area of 5,629 mi (14,580 km). Garhwal rapidly advanced in material prosperity. Two battalions of the Indian army (the 39th Garhwal Rifles) were recruited in the district, which also contained the military cantonment of Lansdowne. Grain and coarse cloth were exported, and salt, borax, livestock and wool were imported, and the trade with Tibetwas considerable. The administrative headquarters were at Pauri, but Srinagar(Garhwal) was the largest city. It was an important mart, as was Kotdwara -the terminus of a branch of the Oudh and Rohilkhand railway from Najibabad. Later it was part of the Punjab Hill States Agency of British India, consisting of the present day Tehri Garhwal district and most of the Uttarkashi district and acceded to the Union of India in 1949.

Language

The Garhwali language is primarily spoken by the Garhwali people of the north-western Garhwal Division from the northern Indian state of Uttarakhand in the Indian Himalayas. The Garhwali language is classified as a Central Pahari language belonging to the Northern Zone of Indo-Aryan languages. Garhwali is one of the 325 recognised languages of India spoken by over 2,267,314 people in Tehri Garhwal, Pauri Garhwal, Uttarkashi, Chamoli, Dehradun, Haridwar and Rudraprayag districts of Uttarakhand.

Garhwali was the official language of the Kingdom of Garhwal since the 8th century. Garhwal was always a semi-sovereign kingdom under the Garhwali Kings. Naturally, Garhwali was the official language of the Garhwal Kingdom for hundreds of years under the Panwar (Shah) Kings and even before them, until the Gurkhas captured Garhwal and subsequently the British occupied part of Garhwal, which later came to be called British Garhwal.

The language has many regional dialects including: Srinagari, Tehri (Gangapariya), Badhani, Dessaulya, Lohbya, Majh-Kumaiya, Bhattiani, Nagpuriya, Rathi, Salani (Pauri), Ravai, Parvati, Jaunpuri, Gangadi (Uttarkashi), Chandpuri. Srinagari dialect is the literary standard while Pauri is generally regarded as the sweetest.

However, due to a number of reasons, Garhwali is one of the languages which is shrinking very rapidly. UNESCO's Atlas of the World's Languages in Danger designates Garhwali as a language which is in the unsafe category and requires consistent conservation efforts.

MUSIC OF UTTARAKHAND

Folk music of Uttarakhand refers to the traditional and contemporary songs of Kumaon and Garhwal regions in the foothills of Himalayas. This music has its root in the lap of nature and the hilly terrain of the region.

The folks songs of Uttarakhand are a reflection of the cultural heritage and the way people live their lives in the Himalayas. Common themes in the folk music of Uttarakhand are the beauty of nature, various seasons, festivals, religious traditions, cultural practices, folk stories, historical characters, the bravery of ancestors and love ballads.

Traditional musical instruments used in Uttarakhandi music include the dhol, damaun, turri, ransingha, dholki, daur, thali, bhankora and mashakbaja. Tabla and harmonium are also sometimes used, especially in recorded folk music from the 1960s onwards. In recent years, Uttarakhandi folk songs have undergone transformation. Generic Indian and global musical instruments have been incorporated in modern popular folks by singers like Narendra Singh Negi, Gopal Babu Goswami, Mohan Upreti, Chander Singh 'Rahi' etc. Modern themes include geo-political issues affecting the region, humour, nostalgia for the hills by the diaspora etc.

Traditional folk songs from the region, include ceremonial mandal, martial panwara, melancholy khuder, religious jagar, thadya and jhora.

Prominent folk artists of Uttarakhand

The earliest of the singers who left never ending impressions on the folk music of Uttarakhand are

1. Narendra Singh Negi : He has sung in every style of singing popular in Uttarakhand be it Jagar, Chaumasa, Thadya or Playback. He has sung in different local languages (boli) like Garhwali, Kumaoni, Jaunsari prevailing in the state. He started his music career by releasing "Garhwali Geetmala". These Garhwali Geetmalas came in 10 different parts. His first album came with the title called "Burans". Burans is a well-known flower found on hills.He has released most number of super-hit albums. He has also given his voice in many Garhwali movies like "Chakrachal", "Gharjawain", "Meri Ganga Holi Ta Maima Aali" etc. This renowned singer from Garhwal has sung more than 1000 songs till now. Although he mostly composes his music in the folk genre, his lyrics depict a huge range of anxieties, tensions and human insights of the people of Uttarakhand. His Song "Tehri Dam" and "Nauchhami Naraina" created a wave. "Tehri Dam" was the story of displacement of locals from their land and Nauchhami Naraina was a political satire on then Chief Minister of Uttarakhand Narayan Datt Tiwari. He is widely considered as an inspirational figure in cultivating and popularizing the sounds and rhythms of Uttarakhand.
2. Mohan Upreti: A famous folk-singer from Kumaon, Mohan Upreti is known for his Nanda Devi Jagar & Rajula Malushahi Ballad.His iconic Kumaoni song *Bedu Pako Baro Masa* is fondly referred to as the cultural anthem of Uttarakhand . It is said that this song was also a favourite of former Prime Minister of India Jawahar Lal Nehru who heard it in a band march as this song is also the official regiment song of the Kumaon Regiment of Indian Army. This iconic song has been covered by various artists and dance groups all over the world.

3. Gopal Babu Goswami who is considered to be a legend in Uttarakhand for his melodious voice. His songs on the life of the members of the armed forces and their families, like *Kaile Baje Muruli, Ghughuti Na Basa* and many others are legendary, it is said that when these songs were transmitted on the All India Radio, women with their husbands working far away from the Uttarakhand hills could not help but weep, missing their husbands when they heard the soul touching voice of *Gopal Da* as he was lovingly called.
4. Chander Singh 'Rahi' fondly called the "Bhishma Pitamaha of Uttarakhand folk music" for his deep devotion to the music of Uttarakhand curated more than 2500 folk songs from Uttarakhand and gave his voice to more than 500 songs of Garhwali and Kumaoni language. He was also a talented musician, poet, and song-writer. He is known for his Uttarakhandi songs including 'Sarag tara', 'Bhana hai rangeeli bhana', 'Sauli ghura ghur', 'Saat samundar paar', 'Hilma chandi ku', and 'Jara thandu chla di'. He was also the first singer to sing a ghazal in Garhwali language known as *Teri Mukhiri*'. Rahi has been an inspiration was for many later Garhwali singers. Garhwali singer Narendra Singh Negi has cited Chandra Singh Rahi as his inspiration. Rahi's popular songs *Phyonlariya* and traditional *Anchari Jagar - Chaita Ki Chaitwali* were remade by popular Garhwali singers in 2016 and 2018 respectively.
5. Basanti Devi Bisht is a famous singer from Uttarakhand specialising in Jagar music.
6. Meena Rana is the most recorded female singer from Uttarakhand.
7. Heera Singh Rana is identified as a singer and a poet of whose songs are known to describe the pain of the people of the hills.

In the past decade Uttarakhandi Music has seen a revolution as various Music Recording/Cassette Producing agencies such as Rama Video Cassettes, Neelam Cassettes and T-Series, provided opportunities for young talents from local areas, to make their own Cassettes and to get the songs recorded in the BIG BOSS digital sound recording studio (at Dehradun, Uttarakhand). This has led to a sudden surge in the number of young talents from various corners of Uttarakhand, which include famous personalities such as Lalit Mohan Joshi, Manglesh Dangwal, Kalpana Chauhan, Anuradha Nirala, Pritam Bharatwan, Gajendra Rana, Arvind Singh Rawat. All these singers have made their contribution to the Kumaoni / Garhwali Music through various hit songs / music albums over the period.

Some famous songs / albums from Uttarakhand include Fauji Lalit Mohan Joshi's "Maya Ki Yaad", "Tak Taka Tak Kamla"; Gajendra Rana's "Malu", "Rani Gorkhani", "Lila Ghasyari", "Pushpa"; Pritam Bharatwan's "Saruli", "Rajuli".

Also, with an advance in the technology and easy availability of video cameras and other recording devices, lots of talents have started producing music albums, which has further led to the popularisation of the various folk dance forms of Uttarakhand. In fact, Kumaoni / Garhwali songs have gained so much popularity over the years that they have become integral part of the DJ Music played during wedding and other functions.

MUSIC AND DANCE

The Himalayas have inspired generations of singers, dancers, and musicians throughout the ages. The natural beauty of the mountains—which inspires a deep spirituality—and the harshness of life—which darkens the heart with adversity and anguish—have invigorated Uttarakhandi music, heightening its poignancy and enriching its lyrical texture.

The Garhwal and Kumaonese are fond of music, folk dance, and songs accompanied by local musical instruments. They go from place to place narrating folklores, dancing and singing the praise of their gods and goddesses. During fairs and festivals and at harvest time, the Kumaonese often dance the Jharva, Chandhur Chhapalior, and many other forms of folk dances.

Major dance forms of the Garhwal region are Langvir Nritya, Barada Nati folk dance, Pandava Nritya, Dhurang, Dhuring and Chhura, Chapeli (folk dances).

MUSIC OF UTTARAKHAND

Music of India: Topics

Bhajan	Bhangra
Filmi	Bhavageete
Lavani	Ghazal
Baul sangeet	Sufi music (Qawwali)

Timeline and Samples

Genres	Classical (Carnatic and Hindustani) - Rock - Pop - Hip hop
Awards	Bollywood Music Awards - Punjabi Music Awards
Charts	
Festivals	Sangeet Natak Akademi – Thyagaraja Aradhana – Cleveland Thyagaraja Aradhana
Media	Sruti, The Music Magazine
National anthem	"Jana Gana Mana", also national song "Vande Mataram"

MUSIC OF THE STATES

Andaman and Nicobar Islands - Andhra Pradesh – Arunachal Pradesh – Assam – Bihar – Chhattisgarh – Goa– Gujarat – Haryana – Himachal Pradesh – Jammu– Jharkhand – Karnataka – Kashmir – Kerala – Madhya Pradesh – Maharashtra – Manipur – Meghalaya – Mizoram– Nagaland – Orissa – Punjab – Rajasthan – Sikkim – Tamil Nadu – Tripura – Uttar Pradesh – Uttarakhand – West Bengal.

Uttarakhand, the 27th state of India, is often referred as the Land of Gods. It is a place blessed with the beauty of heaven and the grace of Gods. This is the place where the rivers passing through the huge rocks and wind passing through large pine trees produces a natural melody by itself.

Uttarakhandi folk music had its root in the lap of nature. The pure and blessed music have the feel and the touch of nature and subjects related to nature. The folk music primarily is related to the various festivals, religious traditions, folk stories and simple life of the people of Uttarakhand. Thus the songs of Uttarakhand are a true reflection of the Cultural Heritage and the way people lives their lives in the Himalayas.

There are many kinds of folk songs from the area, including ceremonial mandals, martial panwaras and melancholy khuded, thadya and jhoda.

Musical instruments used in Uttarakhand music include the dhol, damoun, turri, ransingha, dholki, daur, thali, bhankora and masakbhaja. Tabla and harmonium are also used, but to a lesser extent.

The Music and its development have seen various phases of growth and have undergone lots of transformation during the course of time.

The earliest of the singers who left never ending impressions on the folk music of Uttarakhand were :

1. Shri Narendra Singh Negi who is considered to be the voice of Uttarakhand.
2. Shri Gopal Babu Goswami who is considered to be a legend in Kumaon for his melodious voice.

Other famous personality associated with Kumaoni Folk Music is Mohan Upreti, who is known for his Nanda Devi Jagar & Rajula Malu Shahi Ballad.

Likewise Chander Singh Rahi is another popular singer, a balladeer and storyteller. His recordings are perhaps the most authentic to the hills, and he incorporates many legends and folk tales into his rousing songs.

In the past decade Uttarakhandi Music has seen a revolution

after the offer by various Music Recording/ Cassette Producing agencies such as Rama Video Cassette and T Series who have offered news talents from local areas to make their own Cassettes after getting their songs recorded in the Studios.

This has led to a sudden surge of a number of hidden talents from various corners of Uttarakhand which include famous personalities such as Kalpana Chauhan, Meena Rana, Anuradha Nirala, Fauji Lalit Mohan Joshi, Pritam Bharatwan, Gajendra Rana who have made their contribution to the Garhwali / Kumaoni Music by various hit songs/ music albums over the period.

Some of the hit songs / albums being Gajendra Rana's "Malu", "Rani Gorkhani", "Leel Ghasyari", "Pushpa"; Pritam Bhartwan's "Saruli", "Rajuli"; Fauji Lalit Mohan Joshi's "Maya Ki Yaad", "Tak Taka Kamla" and many other hit albums / songs.

Meena Rana with her melodious voice at present features in almost every second album and can be appropriately called "Lata Mangeshkar of Uttarakhand".

Also, with advance in Technology and easy availability of videocams and other recording devices, lots of talents have started producing music albums which has further led to popularization of Uttarakhandi folk dance. In fact, Garhwali/Kumaoni songs have gained so much popularity over the years that they have become integral part of the DJ Music being played during wedding and other functions.

With the rapid growth and popularity in Uttarakhandi Music and folk dances, the day is not far when any cultural / social functions / weddings / festivals / Discotheques would have some elements of Uttarakhandi Music and folk dances as an integral part.

RANG BHANG

Rang Bhang is one of an interesting custom among the Bhotiya Darma, Chaudangsi and Byangsi tribes of Kali-Kuthi valley, Pithoragarh district of Uttarakhand, India. It is like the night club of marriageable young boys and girls. Celebrations go on till whole night till most of them found suitable partner. This tradition is slowly dying.

CULTURE AND SOCIETY

The history of modern Garhwal/Kumaon dates back to 7th and 8th Century AD when the Yavans began capturing the plains of India. Most of then Hindu kings from various parts of India migrated to Uttarakhand along with their family, army and the priests. Later on the children of the armymen and the priests contributed to the population of the region. As a result of this migration, the Uttarakhand society consists of 70% Rajputs, 20% Brahamans and the remaining 10% comprises of other castes and communites. Since kings from various parts of India migrated to Uttarakhand, the Uttarakhand culture reflects the diverse culture of every region.

The presence of Rajput majority in the region contributed to the worship of the Godess of Power - "Durga" which is still practised in almost every part of Uttarakhand. The fact gets proven with the presence of various Durga temples across the region. The animal sacrifice was also a part of this worship and still practised in many regions.

The antiquity of the sate can be traced back to 2nd century BC when the region was ruled by the Khasias and it was known as Khashdesh. Recent excavations has indicated that the region was under the domain of Kunidas, the central Himalayan tribe, who practiced early form of Shaivism at around 200 AD. There is also an Ashokan edict at Kalsi, in Garhwal region, which indicates that Buddhism also reached these parts of the country.

Between the 10th and 18th centuries, the Chand dynasty dominated the eastern Kumaon. Under the Chands, eastern Kumaon became a centre of learning, and various art forms including Garhwal school of painting was developed. With the decline of the Chand dynasty the region became under the Garhwali kings till the Rohillas took charge of the land in 1744 AD.

The area was overtaken by Gurkhas in 1803 and ultimately

by the end of 1814, Britishers expelled Gurkhas from Garhwal and Kumaon to take eastern Garhwal as British Garhwal and returned the western part, Tehri Garhwal to the deposed Raja. After 1857, the region became part of British empire. Since independence, the local aspiration steadily grew demanding a separate state of Uttarakhand which finally acquired its dream of statehood on 9th November 2000. The region is presently subsisting on the tourism business. It is also the land of the brave. Its Garhwalis and Kumaonis are reputed to the finest soldiers of our armed forces.

GARHWALI CULTURE

Garhwal, or Gadhwal, is a region and administrative division of Uttarakhand, lying in the Himalayas. It is bounded on the north by Tibet, on the east by Kumaon region, on the south by Uttar Pradesh, and on the west by Himachal Pradesh. It includes the districts of Chamoli, Dehradun, Haridwar, Pauri (Pauri Garhwal), Rudraprayag, Tehri (Tehri Garhwal), and Uttarkashi. The administrative centre for Garhwal division is the town of Pauri.

The region consists almost entirely of rugged mountain ranges running in all directions, and separated by narrow valleys which in some cases become deep gorges or ravines. The only level portion of the district was a narrow strip of waterless forest between the southern slopes of the hills and the fertile plains of Rohilkhand. The highest mountains are in the north, the principal peaks being Nanda Devi (25,661 feet), Kamet (25,413 feet), Trisul (23,382 feet), Badrinath (23,210 feet), Dunagiri (23,181 feet) and Kedarnath (22,853 feet). The Alaknanda River, one of the main sources of the Ganges, receives with its affluents the whole drainage of the district. At Devaprayag the Alaknanda joins the Bhagirathi, and thenceforward the united streams bear the name of the Ganges. Cultivation is principally confined to the immediate vicinity of the rivers, which are employed for purposes of irrigation.

Garhwal originally consisted of 52 petty chieftainships, each chief with his own independent fortress (garh). Nearly 500 years ago, one of these chiefs, Ajai Pal, reduced all the minor principalities under his own sway, and founded the Garhwal kingdom. He and his ancestors ruled over Garhwal and the adjacent state of Tehri, in an uninterrupted line till 1803, when the Gurkhas invaded Kumaon and Garhwal, driving the Garhwal chief into the plains. For twelve years the Gurkhas ruled the country with a rod of iron, until a series of encroachments by them on British territory led to the war with Nepal in 1814. At the termination of the campaign, Garhwal and Kumaon were converted into British districts, while the Tehri principality was restored to a son of the former chief.

The British district of Garhwal was in the Kumaon division of the United Provinces, and had an area of 5629 sq. mi. After annexation, Garhwal rapidly advanced in material prosperity. Pop. (1901) 429,900.

Two battalions of the Indian army (the 39th Garhwal Rifles) were recruited in the district, which also contained the military cantonment of Lansdowne. Grain and coarse cloth were exported, and salt, borax, livestock and wool were imported, and the trade with Tibet was considerable.

The administrative headquarters was at the village of Pauri, but Srinagar is the largest place. It was an important mart, as was Kotdwara, the terminus of a branch of the Oudh and Rohilkhand railway from Najibabad.

UTTARAKHAND SWAR-SANGAM

"Uttarakhand Swar-Sangam" is a cultural forum. All the active participants/ members of the society belong to Uttarakhand that too mostly from Kumaon Region. We have been organising famous folk arts, Chhura, Chapeli & other cultural dances for last 4 years in Lucknow, in different parts of UP and in other states.

Chhura: Chhura dance is very popular among the people and is in a way of an old experienced man teaching a young Shepherd the tricks of his trade. Both men and women participate in this dance.

Chapeli: It is a very famous and fast dance of Kumaon. The theme of the dance is love and it is very romantic. Both men and women participate in this dance and the costume is very colourful.

Chitai: Chitai is a place on the Almora-Pithoragarh highway, six kms from Almora towns in the Uttarakhand state of India. This place is famous for the temple of Golu Devata or Lord Golu. This place is situated among beautiful natural surroundings rich with Pine trees.

3

Government and Politics

GOVERNMENT OF UTTARAKHAND

The Government of Uttarakhand also known as the State Government of Uttarakhand, or locally as State Government, is the supreme governing authority of the Indian state of Uttarakhand and its 13 Districts. It consists of an executive branch, led by the Governor of Uttarakhand, a judiciary branch, led by the Chief Justice of Uttarakhand and a legislative branch led by the Chief Minister of Uttarakhand.

Like other states in India, the head of state of Uttarakhand is the Governor, appointed by the President of India on the advice of the Central government. His or her post is largely ceremonial. The Chief Minister is the head of government and is vested with most of the executive powers. Currently Dehradun is the capital of Uttarakhand, and houses the Vidhan Sabha (Legislative Assembly) and the Secretariat. The Uttarakhand High Court, located in Nainital exercises jurisdiction over the whole state.

The present unicameral legislature of Uttarakhand is the Legislative Assembly of Uttarakhand. It comprises 71 Members of Legislative Assembly (MLAs). 70 seats are for free elections and 1 seat is reserved for a member of Anglo Indian community, whom the Governor of Uttarakhand Appoints on the consent of Chief Minister of Uttarakhand. Assembly's term is 5 years, unless sooner dissolved.

GOVERNMENT AND POLITICS

Following the Constitution of India, Uttarakhand, like all Indian states, has a parliamentary system of representative democracy for its government.

The Governor is the constitutional and formal head of the government and is appointed for a five-year term by the President of India on the advice of the Union government. The present Governor of Uttarakhand is Baby Rani Maurya. The Chief Minister, who holds the real executive powers, is the head of the party or coalition garnering the majority in the state elections. The current Chief Minister of Uttarakhand is Trivendra Singh Rawat. The unicameral Uttarakhand Legislative Assembly consists of has 71 elected members, known as Members of the Legislative Assembly or MLAs, and special office bearers such as the Speaker and Deputy Speaker, elected by the members. Assembly meetings are presided over by the Speaker, or the Deputy Speaker in the Speaker's absence. A Council of Ministers is appointed by the Governor of Uttarakhand on the advice of the Chief Minister of Uttarakhand and reports to the Legislative Assembly. Auxiliary authorities that govern at a local level are known as panchayats in rural areas, municipalities in urban areas and municipal corporation in metro areas. All state and local government offices have a five-year term. The state also elects 5 members to Lok Sabha and 3 seats to Rajya Sabha of the Indian Parliament. The judiciary consists of the Uttarakhand High Court, located at Nainital, and a system of lower courts. The incumbent Acting Chief Justice of Uttarakhand is Justice Rajiv Sharma.

Politics in Uttarakhand is dominated by the Indian National Congress and the Bharatiya Janata Party. Since the formation of the state these parties have ruled the state in turns. Following the hung mandate in the Uttarakhand Legislative Assembly election, 2012, the Indian National Congress, having the maximum number of seats, formed a coalition government headed by Harish Rawat that collapsed on 27 March 2016, following the political turmoil as about nine MLAs of INC rebelled against the party and supported the opposition party BJP, causing Harish Rawat government to lose the majority in assembly. However, on 21 April 2016 the High Court of Uttarakhand quashed the President's Rulequestioning its legality and maintained a status quo prior to 27 March 2016 when 9 rebel MLAs of INC voted against the Harish Rawatgovernment in assembly on state's money appropriation bill. This has been seen as a big blow to central government which is expected to take the matter to the Supreme Court of India to challenge the verdict of High Court. On 22 April 2016 the Supreme Court of India stayed the order of High Court till 27 April 2016, thereby once again reviving the President's Rule. In later developments regarding this matter, the Supreme Court ordered a floor test to be held on 10 May with the rebels being barred from voting. On 11 May at the opening of sealed result of the floor test, under the supervision of Supreme Court, the Harish Rawat government was revived following the victory in floor test held in Uttarakhand Legislative Assembly.

Following the 2017 Legislative Assembly election, on 18 March 2017 Trivendra Singh Rawat sworn as the 8th Chief Minister of Uttarakhand of Fourth Assembly (2017–22).

Sub-divisions

There are 13 districts in Uttarakhand which are grouped into two divisions, Kumaon and Garhwal. Four new districts named Didihat, Kotdwar Ranikhet, and Yamunotri were declared by then Chief Minister of Uttarakhand, Ramesh Pokhriyal, on 15 August 2011 but yet to be officially formed.

Each district is governed by a district collector or district magistrate. The districts are further divided into sub-divisions, which are governed by sub-divisional magistrates; sub-divisions comprise blocks containing panchayats (village councils) and town municipalities.

According to the 2011 census, Haridwar, Dehradun, and

Udham Singh Nagar are the most populous districts, each of them having a population of over one million.

LIST OF GOVERNORS OF UTTARAKHAND

The governor of Uttarakhand is appointed by the President of India for a term of five years, and holds office at the President's pleasure. The governor is *de jure* head of the state government; all its executive actions are taken in the governor's name. However, the governor must act on the advice of the popularly elected Cabinet of Uttarakhand, headed by the Chief Minister of Uttarakhand, who thus hold *de facto* executive authority at the state-level. The Constitution of India also empowers the governor to act upon his or her own discretion, such as the ability to appoint or dismiss a ministry, recommend President's rule, or reserve bills for the President's assent. The governor of Uttarakhand has his official residence at the Raj Bhavan in the state capital of Dehradun.

Uttarakhand was created on 9 November 2000, when it was carved out from the himalayan districts of Uttar Pradesh. Seven people have served as the state's governor, five are men and two women including the incumbent Baby Rani Maurya.

Powers and functions

The governor enjoys many different types of powers:

- Executive powers related to administration, appointments and removals,
- Legislative powers related to lawmaking and the state legislature, that is Vidhan Sabha(legislative assembly) & vidhan parishad, and
- Discretionary powers to be carried out according to the discretion of the governor.

CHIEF MINISTERS OF UTTARAKHAND

The Chief Minister of the State of Uttarakhand, is the head of the Government of Uttarakhand. As per the Constitution of India, the Governor of Uttarakhand is the state's *de jure* head, but *de facto* executive authority rests with the chief minister.

Following elections to the Uttarakhand Legislative Assembly, the governor usually invites the party (or coalition) with a majority of seats to form the government. The governor appoints the chief minister, whose council of ministers are collectively responsible to the assembly. Given that he has the confidence of the assembly, the chief minister's term is for five years and is subject to no term limits.

Uttarakhand was formed on November 9, 2000, when it was carved out from the himalayan districts of Uttar Pradesh. Eight people have served as the state's chief minister, across five assembly terms; five of those belong to the Bharatiya Janata Party including the current incumbent Trivendra Singh Rawat and the inaugural office holder Nityanand Swami, while the remaining three belong to the Indian National Congress.

UTTARAKHAND COUNCIL OF MINISTERS

The Uttarakhand Council of Ministers is the executive wing of Government of Uttarakhand and headed by Chief Minister of Uttarakhand, who is the head of government and leader of the state cabinet. The term of every executive wing is for 5 years. The council of ministers are assisted by department secretaries attached to each ministry who are from IAS Uttarakhand Cadre. The chief executive officer responsible for issuing orders on behalf of government is Chief Secretary to the state government. The current Chief Secretary is Utpal Kumar Singh who took charge from outgoing S. Ramaswamy on 25 October, 2017.

Constitutional requirement

For the Council of Ministers to aid and advise Governor

According to Article 163 of the Indian Constitution,

1. "There shall be a Council of Ministers with the Chief Minister at the head to aid and advise the Governor in the exercise of his function, except in so far as he is by or under this Constitution required to exercise his functions or any of them in his discretion.

2. If any question arises whether any matter is or is not a matter as respects which the Governor is by or under this Constitution required to act in his discretion, the decision of the Governor in his discretion shall be final, and the validity of anything done by the Governor shall not be called in question on the ground that he ought or ought not to have acted in his discretion.

The question whether any, and if so what, advice was tendered by Ministers to the Governor shall not be inquired into in any court. "

This means that the Ministers serve under the pleasure of the Governor and he/she may remove them, on the advice of the Chief Minister, whenever they want.

For other provisions as to Ministers

According to Article 164 of the Indian Constitution,

1. "The Chief Minister shall be appointed by the Governor and the other Ministers shall be appointed by the Governor on the advice of the Chief Minister, and the Minister shall hold office during the pleasure of the Governor:
2. Provided that in the States of Bihar, Madhya Pradesh and Orissa, there shall be a Minister in charge of tribal welfare who may in addition be in charge of the welfare of the Scheduled Castes and backward classes or any other work.
3. The Council of Minister shall be collectively responsible to the Legislative Assembly of the State.
4. Before a Minister enters upon his office, the Governor shall administer to him the oaths of office and of secrecy according to the forms set out for the purpose in the Third Schedule.
5. A Minister who for any period of six consecutive months is not a member of the Legislature of the State shall at the expiration of that period cease to be a Minister.

The salaries and allowances of Ministers shall be such as the

Legislature of the State may from time to time by law determine and, until the Legislature of the State so determines, shall be a specified in the Second Schedule."

Chief Minister

Like any Indian state, Chief Ministers of Uttarakhand is the real head of the government and responsible for state administration. He is the leader of the parliamentary party in the legislature and heads the state cabinet. The current Chief Minister is Trivendra Singh Rawat.

State Cabinet

As per Indian Constitution, all portfolios of state government is vested in Chief Minister, who distribute various portfolio to individual ministers whom he nominates to the State Governor. The state governor appoints individual ministers for various portfolios and departments as per advice of Chief Minister and together form the State Cabinet. As the original portfolios are vested with CM, who delegates to others upon his/her wish, actions of individual ministers are part of collective responsibility of the state cabinet and Chief Minister is responsible for actions of each minister. The state cabinet along with Chief Minister, prepares General policy and individual department policy, which will be guiding policy for day-to-day administration of each minister.

UTTARAKHAND HIGH COURT

The Uttarakhand High Court is the High Court of the state of Uttarakhand in India. The Uttarakhand State was carved out from the State of Uttar Pradesh on 9 November 2000 under the Uttar Pradesh Reorganisation Act, 2000. At the time of the creation of the State, the High Court of Uttarakhand was also established on the same day at Nainital.

The sanctioned judge strength at the time of creation in 2000 was 7; this was increased to 9 in 2003. Justice Ashok A. Desai was the inaugural holder of the office. Former Chief Justices of Uttarakhand S. H. Kapadia and J. S. Khehar later went on to become Chief Justice of India. Ramesh Ranganathan is the current Chief Justice of the Uttarakhand High Court. He assumed office on 25 October 2018.

Registrar General

Pradeep Pant is the Registrar General of the Uttarakhand High Court. He Assumed office on 16 August 2018.

UTTARAKHAND LEGISLATIVE ASSEMBLY

The Uttarakhand Legislative Assembly, also known as the Uttarakhand Vidhan Sabha, is a unicameral governing and law making body of Uttarakhand, one of the 29 States in India, and is situated at Dehradun, the interim state capital of Uttarakhand, with 71 Members of the Legislative Assembly (MLA).

Following the Bharatiya Janta Party's historic win in 2017 election, the current Chief Minister of Uttarakhand and Leader of the House is Trivendra Singh Rawat. The Speaker of the Assembly is Premchand Aggarwal. Baby Rani Maurya is the current Governor of Uttarakhand. From 27 March 2016 to 12 May 2016, Uttarakhand was under President's Rule.

Suspension

Capping a nine-day high-voltage political drama, the Central Government on Sunday brought Uttarakhand under President's rule citing a constitutional breakdown in the wake of a rebellion in the ruling Congress, which slammed the decision calling it a "murder of democracy" and a "black" day.

President Pranab Mukherjee signed the proclamation under Article 356 of the Constitution dismissing the Congress government headed by Harish Rawat and placing the Assembly under suspended animation this morning on the recommendation of the Union Cabinet.

The Central Government was of the view that continuance of the Rawat government was "immoral and unconstitutional" after the 18 March 2016, when the Speaker declared the Appropriation Bill "passed" in controversial circumstances without allowing a division pressed for by 35 MLAs, including 9 rebel Congress legislators.

The Union Cabinet had held an emergency meeting on Saturday night presided over by Prime Minister Narendra Modi, who had cut short a visit to Assam to return to the capital for the purpose.

The Cabinet considered several reports received from Governor K. K. Paul, who had described the political situation as volatile and expressed apprehensions over possible pandemonium during the scheduled trial of strength in the State Assembly on Monday.

The purported CD of the sting operation conducted against the Chief Minister that was in public domain on Saturday was understood to have been factored into the decision of the Cabinet which found it as a case of horse trading.

Additionally Two Uttarakhand MLAs, one each from Indian National Congress and Bharatiya Janata Party were on 9 June suspended for cross-voting during the floor test that was held on 10 May. Uttarakhand Assembly Speaker Govind Singh Kunjwalsuspended BJP MLA Bhim Lal Arya and INC MLA Rekha Arya.

ELECTIONS IN UTTARAKHAND

Elections for the Uttarakhand Legislative Assembly in Uttarakhand state, India are conducted in accordance with the Constitution of India. The Assembly of Uttarakhand creates laws regarding the conduct of local body elections unilaterally while any changes by the state legislature to the conduct of state level elections need to be approved by the Parliament of India. In addition, the state legislature may be dismissed by the Parliament according to Article 356 of the Indian Constitution and President's rule may be imposed.

Main Political Parties

The Bharatiya Janata Party and Indian National Congress have been the most popular parties in the state since its inception. Other influential parties include Samajwadi Party,

Bahujan Samaj Party and Uttarakhand Kranti Dal.

Lok Sabha Elections

It is worth noting that till the year 2000, Uttarakhand was a part of undivided Uttar Pradesh state.

Year	Lok Sabha Election	Party-wise Details
2004	14th Lok Sabha	Total: 5. BJP: 3, Congress: 1 and Samajwadi Party:1.
2009	15th Lok Sabha	Total: 5. Congress: 5, BJP: 0.
2014	16th Lok Sabha	Total: 5. BJP: 5, Congress: 0.

1st Assembly Election 2002

Uttarakhand Legislative Assembly elections, 2002 were the first Vidhan Sabha (Legislative Assembly) elections held in the state. The Indian National Congress emerged as the largest party with 36 seats in the 70-seat legislature whereas the Bharatiya Janata Party secured the second place with 19 seats. Veteran Congress leader N. D. Tiwari was chosen as the new Chief minister.

2nd Assembly Election 2007

Uttarakhand state assembly elections, 2007 were the second Vidhan Sabha (Legislative Assembly) elections held in the state. The Bharatiya Janata Party emerged as the single largest party with 34 seats in the 70-seat legislature. One seat short of forming a majority, the BJP had to rely on the support of the Uttarakhand Kranti Dal and three independents to form the government. Former Union minister B C Khanduri became the new Chief minister. The Indian National Congress was the official opposition, holding 21 seats.

3rd Assembly Election 2012

Uttarakhand had turned out incumbent governments in the first two elections held in the state since its formation. The ruling Bharatiya Janata Party fought the election under the leadership of its Chief Minister B C Khanduri. The main opposition Indian National Congress was led in the assembly by Harak Singh Rawat, but no Chief Ministerial candidate was named before the elections. The interim tenure of former Chief Minister Ramesh Pokhriyal, which was marked by large-scale corruption accusations, was likely to be the main election issue.

The elections took place on 30 January, with the results being announced on 6 March. In a closely contested election, the Indian National Congress emerged as the single largest party with 32 seats followed by the Bharatiya Janata Party with 31 seats. Notably the incumbent Chief minister BC Khanduri lost from his seat. Vijay Bahuguna was appointed as Chief minister despite him not being a member of the legislative assembly. He later on won the byelections held to the seats of Sitarganj. The detailed result is given below:

4th Assembly Election 2017

Uttarakhand state assembly elections, 2017 were the fourth Vidhan Sabha (Legislative Assembly) elections held in the state. The Bharatiya Janata Party riding on the popularity of Prime minister Narendra Modi, secured a landslide victory, winning 57 of the total 70 seats. The ruling Indian National Congress was reduced to a low of 11 seats, with the incumbent Chief minister Harish Rawat himself losing from both the seats that he had contested from. Although the BJP had not projected anyone as its Chief ministerial candidate, Trivendra Singh Rawat was chosen as the new Chief minister after the elections.

4

Language and Literature

LANGUAGES OF UTTARAKHAND

Uttarakhand, the *devbhoomi* of India or the land of gods is a beautiful northern state nestled in the Himalayas. People from across the nation flock to Uttarakhand, mainly to enjoy the fresh mountain air and get away from the hassle of city life. This northern state is also popular for its various treks that take one through the snow-clad mountains, meadows, lush green forests and offer spectacular views of the Himalayan ranges.

Uttarakhand has a rich history which can be traced back to the Vedic age and today is home to various communities and tribes, each having their own distinct culture. Music and dance is an integral part of this culture. This state is broadly divided into two parts, Kumaon and Garhwal region but in these regions, one can also find various tribes like Tharu, Jannsari, Bhotia, among others. Uttarakhand is home to people of multiple ethnicities who speak multiple languages. Although the main languages Uttarakhand is associated with are Garhwali and Kumaoni, but these are not the official languages of the state. Mentioned below are some of the major languages of Uttarakhand.

Hindi

Hindi is one of the major languages of Uttarakhand and is spoken by the majority of the population. In the recent year, the state has seen a rise in the Hindi speaking population, making it the highest the state has seen, around 88.26% of the total population.

Hindi is the official language of the state of Uttarakhand, and even the illiterate can understand this language. Hindi is also one of the official languages of India as recognised by the Eighth Schedule of the Constitution. It is taught in schools and is used as a medium to teach other subjects as well. Even in the schools located in the remote areas of Uttarakhand, Hindi is the language in use. Although it isn't the mother tongue of the people living in the remote regions of Garhwal or Kumaon, it is the one they are educated in.

Sanskrit

Sanskrit is mostly read in texts and taught in schools. This ancient language is no longer in popular use or has any practical purposes, but it is an important language in which other languages are rooted. Although Sanskrit isn't a language which is used by people to interact on a daily basis, it has been given the status of the second official language of Uttarakhand.

Although many of us might not even remember Sanskrit, it is taught as a compulsory subject in schools. Even in Uttarakhand, children learn to read and write this language in schools. Now, it also being considered to introduce this language in *madrasas*.

Garhwali

Garhwali is a regional language which is spoken in the northwestern Garhwal region of Uttarakhand. The language has many dialects like Srinagariya, Badhani, Tehri, Lohbya, Jaunsari etc. which differ from one another. For instance, people in Tehri Garhwal and Pauri Garhwal speak a different type of Garhwali which often is hard to understand by the people of other community.

Garhwali belongs to the Indo-Aryan languages. It is often the first language of the Garhwali community living in Uttarakhand, although they do understand Hindi. One can find a lot of migrant Garhwali speaking population in Delhi and National Capital Region. It is spoken by over 22 lakh people in India as per the Census.

Garhwali has mostly been existent as a spoken language that was passed on from one generation to another, verbally. Even the culture consisted of folklore, folk songs which were told verbally. Today, one can find Garhwali prevalent in the form of songs. It has been popularised through folk songs, the most well known being *Bedu Pako*and folk singers like Narendra Singh Negi. Apart from Uttarakhand, Garhwali language has even been established in cities like Delhi and Mumbai where Garhwali Kavi Sammelans have been hosted.

Kumaoni

Kumaoni is another dominant regional language of the state of Uttarakhand. It is a Central Pahari language like Garhwali. It is spoken by people belonging to the Kumaon region. As per the Census, there are around 20 lakh people in India, whose mother tongue is Kumaoni.

As Garhwali, there are regional dialects in Kumaoni although they do not differ much from one another. They can be broadly categorised according to the region as central Kumaoni in Almora and Nainital, north-eastern Kumaoni in Pithoragarh, and southeastern Kumaoni in the south-eastern part of Nainital.

Kumaoni language uses the Devanagari script and follows the same rules of grammar as other Indo-Aryan languages. Kumaon has a rich culture which is reflected in its literature, theatre and folk music. Today, Kumaoni speaking population is declining, and the government needs to put in efforts to conserve this language.

Jaunsari

Jaunsari is a language which is spoken by the Jaunsari tribal community of Uttarakhand. It is a Western Pahari language and is spoken by 1 lakh people in India. The Jaunsari tribe is found in the Jaunsar-Bawar region of Dehradun district and is considered a scheduled tribe as per the Constitution of India. This tribe believes themselves to be the descendants of the Pandavas of the Mahabharata. Jaunsari language is regarded as a dialect of Garhwali language, but it listed as another language because Jaunsari is a significant tribal community of Uttarakhand. Today, Jaunsari is a "definitely endangered" language as per the UNESCO Atlas of the World's Languages in Danger.

Urdu

Uttarakhand is also home to Urdu speaking population which comes down to 5.88%, as per the 2011 Census. Urdu is one of the 22 official languages of India as per the Eighth Schedule of the Constitution. Urdu speakers are a minority group in Uttarakhand. One can find them not in the remote regions of the mountains but cities like Haridwar.

Uttarakhand is a multilingual state which is home to a people of various communities. Today, there are a lot of migrants who have shifted to this Himalayan state either for business or pleasure, thus increasing the diversity of Uttarakhand. In the recent years, the population of Punjabi, Bengali and even Nepali speakers has seen a rise. The above mentioned were some of the significant official or regional languages of Uttarakhand.

LITERATURE

Below we're specifying the complete list of popular writers and authors of Uttarakhand. These personalities actually belong to Uttarakhand state but you can find their presence not only nationwide but worldwide as well. Majorities of stories, poems, and articles are written by them which have earned incredible popularity amongst reader. Go through their complete biography, including family background, education, written stories or articles, awards and achievements etc at our portal. Details mentioned here are collected from numerous resources and our teams have filtered it so that readers would get best possible knowledge about them.

GARHWALI LANGUAGE

Garhwali is the main language (BOLI) spoken in Garhwal. It is one of the languages of the central Pahari language group of the Himalaya. Languages of this group are spoken in the eastern parts of Himachal Pradesh and Garhwal. In turn, Garhwali has a number of dialects which are variations of the main languages-

1. Jaunsari of the people of Jaunsar-Babar and the adjoining tracts
2. Marchi or Bhotia dialect of the Marchas
3. Jadhi or dialect of parts of Uttarkashi
4. Sailani or dialect of parts of Tehri.

INFLUENCE OF OTHER LANGUAGES AND DIALECTS

Many languages and dialects have had an effect on the Garhwali language. These are:

1. Bhotia dialect of Tibet and China
2. Sanskrit, or Hindi, or Hindustani, that is spoken in the areas to the south of Garhwal.

3. Kumaoni and Nepali spoken in the area to the east of Garhwal.
4. Languages and dialects of the western Pahari group that is spoken by the people living in the adjoining tracts of Himachal Pradesh.

The influence of these languages and dialects have been found on the Garhwali language because the people speaking them have moved across the borders of various regions and settled in Garhwal. In turn, the people of Garhwal, too, have moved to these areas picking up influences of the language spoken there, gradually incorporating them into Garhwali.

KUMAONI LANGUAGE

The Kumaoni language is a Central Pahari language.

Kumaoni was spoken by over 2,360,000 (1998) people but it decreased to 2,011,286 (2011) in Uttarakhand, primarily in districts Almora, Nainital, Pithoragarh, Bageshwar, Champawat, Udham Singh Nagar as well as in areas of Himachal Pradesh and Nepal. It is also spoken by Kumaonis resident in other Indian states; Uttar Pradesh, Assam, Bihar, Delhi and Madhya Pradesh.

The Central Pahari languages include Kumaoni and Garhwali (spoken in the Garhwal region of Uttarakhand). Kumaoni, like Garhwali, has many regional dialects spoken in different places in Uttarakhand. Amongst its dialects, the Central Kumauni is spoken in Almora and northern Nainital, Northeastern Kumauni is in Pithoragarh, Southeastern Kumauni is in Southeastern Nainital, Western Kumauni is west of Almora and Nainital.

Almost all people who can speak and understand Kumaoni can also speak and understand Hindi, one of the official languages of India. Due to a number of reasons (including the predominance of Hindi), the use of Kumaoni is shrinking very rapidly. UNESCO's Atlas of the World's Languages in Danger designates Kumaoni as language in the *unsafe* category and which requires consistent conservation efforts.

Dialects of the Kumaoni language

Although dialects of Kumaoni do not vary as greatly as neighboring Garhwali dialects, there are several dialects spoken in the Kumaon region.

There is not single accepted method of dividing up the dialects of Kumaoni. Broadly speaking, Kali (or Central) Kumaoni is spoken in Almora and northern Nainital. North-eastern Kumaoni is spoken in Pithoragarh. South-eastern Kumaoni is spoken in South-eastern Nainital. Western Kumaoni is spoken west of Almora and Nainital.

More specifically:

- Johari of the Johar Valley
- Askoti of Askot
- Bhabhri of Ramnagar
- Chaugarkhiyali of Chaugarkha
- Danpuriya of Danpur
- Gangoli of Ganai-Gangoli (Gangolihat)
- Johari of Malla and Talla Johar
- Khasparjiya of Almora
- Kumaiyya of Champawat
- Pachhai of Pali-Pachhhau (Ranikhet, Dwarahat)
- Pashchimi
- Phaldakotiya of Phaldkot
- Rhau-Chaubyansi, (Nainital)
- Sirali of Sirakot (Didihat)
- Soriyali of Sor Valley (Pithoragarh)
- Sinjali of Jumla Valley (Nepal)
- Palpali of Palpa,Nepal.
- Baitada of Baitadi, Darchula and parts of Bajhang District in Nepal
- Dotiyali of Doti, Nepal

Scholars believe that Kumaoni has heavily influenced the Palpa language of Nepal. There are also several unrelated

Tibeto-Burman languages spoken in the Kumaon region which have had some influence from Kumaoni.

- Rang or Rung
- Darmyali
- Bangbani

These languages are typically spoken in Upper Reaches of Kumaon Himalayas.

Grammar

Being part of the Indo-Aryan dialect continuum Kumauni shares its grammar with other Indo-Aryan languages, especially Nepali, Hindi, Rajasthani languages, Kashmiri and Gujarati. It shares much of its grammar with the other languages of the Central Pahari like Garhwali and Jaunsari. The peculiarities of grammar in Kumaoni and other Central Pahari languages exist due to the influence of the now extinct language of the Khasas, the first inhabitants of the region. In Kumauni the verb substantive is formed from the root ach, as in both Rajasthani and Kashmiri. In Rajasthani its present tense, being derived from the Sanskrit present *rcchami*, I go, does not change for gender. But in Pahari and Kashmiri it must be derived from the rare Sanskrit particle **rcchitas*, gone, for in these languages it is a participial tense and does change according to the gender of the subject. Thus, in the singular we have: - Here we have a relic of the old Khasa language, which, as has been said, seems to have been related to Kashmiri. Other relics of Khasa, again agreeing with north-western India, are the tendency to shorten long vowels, the practice of epenthesis, or the modification of a vowel by the one which follows in the next syllable, and the frequent occurrence of disaspiration. Thus, Khas siknu, Kumauni *sikhno*, but Hindi *sikhna*, to learn; Kumauni *yeso*, plural *yasa*, of this kind.

Kumaoni literature

Kumaoni language has had many noteworthy writers, prominent among them are

- Shailesh Matiyani (1931–2001)
- Mohan Upreti (1925–1997)

Media and art

Films

- *Megha Aa*, (First Kumaoni Film). Director Kaka Sharma, Produced S S Bisht, 1987
- *Teri Saun*, (First film both in Kumaoni and Garhwali), written, produced, and directed by Anuj Joshi, 2003.
- *Aapun Biraan* (Apne Paraye) by Shri Kartikey Cine Productions. Written by Rajendra Bora (*Tribhuvan Giri*). Produced by *Bhaskar Singh Rawat.* 2007.
- *Madhuli* by Anamika Film, 2008.
- *Aapke Liye*, a 1985 TV show aired in Doordarshan Directed by sharbat sanzarr and presented by Mohan Manral showcases the kumaoni mela "kauteek".

Folk music

Folk song genres include ceremonial mandals, martial panwaras and melancholy khuded, thadya and jhoda.

Musical instruments used in Kumaon music include the dhol, damoun, turri, ransingha, dholki, daur, thali, bhankora and masakbhaja. Tabla and harmonium are also used, but to a lesser extent.

Some prominent singers are:

- Mohan Upreti, the most famous personality associated with Kumaoni folk music, who is known for his Nanda Devi Jagar & Rajula Malu Shahi Ballad. He is famous for the great Kumaoni song Bedu Pako Baro Masa which for many years the identity of the hills of Uttarakahand. It is said this song was also a favourite of Pandit Jawahar Lal Nehru who heard it in a band march as this song is also apopular marching song.
- Naima Khan Upreti - She was the wife of Mohan Upreti and was a prominent folk singer. Mohan Upreti and

Naima Upreti used to sing folk songs as a duet and they also made the first HMV recording of songs like Bedu Pako and O Lali, O Lali Haushiya. Naima Upreti had collected a large number of songs of the Kumaon and Garhwal region and she rendered them on several occasions.

- Shri Gopal Babu Goswami who is considered to be a legend in Kumaon for his melodious voice. His songs on the life of the members of the armed forces and their families like Kaile baje muruli, Ghughuti na basa (Hirda cassettes) and many others are legendary, it is said that when these songs were transmitted on All India Radio women could not help but weep when they heard the soul touching voice of Gopal Da as he was lovingly called.
- Heera Singh Rana is identified as a contemporary poet and singer who touched upon various shades of hill life, particularly the plight of women. Besides beauty, love, and romance, his poetry illustrates pains and sufferings and are sharp in satire on the political class.

In the early 90's songs on the turning life style mainly on the one who are heading towards town being made in which meri kumau ki gaadi, hit meri punjaban billo uttarakhand pahara, bwaari tamaaku pija etc. criticize the changing attitude in kumaoni society, the songs of mohan manral straight away criticize of the changing mindset of metropolitan kumaoni society running away from their roots.

Radio

- In 1962, a new programme was introduced from Akashwani Lucknow- "Utterayana". this programme was specially for the Chinese border area. Jay dev sharma "kamal" Banshidhar Pathak Jigyasu and Jeet Singh Jardhari started this programme. Najeebabad Akashwani kendra relayed this programme .
- With the aim to create a common platform for local communities of Supi in Uttarakhand, TERI launched

'Kumaon vani', a community radio service on 11 March 2010. UttarakhandGovernor Margaret Alva inaugurated the community radio station, the first in the state. The 'Kumaon Vani' aims to air programmes on environment, agriculture, culture, weather and education in the local language and with the active participation of the communities. The radio station covers a radius of 10 km reaching out to almost 2000 locals around Mukhteshwar

- In order to create a folk genome tank of Uttarakhand where one can find each genre and occasions in the form of folk music, and to bring the melodious folk from the heart of Himalaya on global screen, the very first internet radio of Kumaon/Garhwal/Jaunsar was launched in year 2008 by a group of non resident Uttarakhandi from New York, which has been gaining significant popularity among inhabitants and migrants since its beta version was launched in year 2010. This was named after a very famous melody of hills of Himalaya, Bedupako Baramasa O Narain Kafal Pako Chaita Bedupako

KUMAONI LANGUAGE AND LITERATURE

Languages Which Are Spoken At Kumaoni Region Belong To Aryan Family; However Dialects Of The Tibeto (Burmese Family) Are Also Used In Some Cases. Less Influence Of Kols, Kinnar-Kirats, Munds, Dard-Khasas Can Also Be Seen In These Dialects. Hindi, That Is The Mother Language Of India Is

Spoken By Almost Every Kumaonis Excluding Biyans And Chaudans, Shaukas Of Darma And The Banrajis Of Askot And Chalthi. There Are 13 Dialects In Kumaon Is Described By G.A.Grierson; They Are: Johari, Danpuriya, Majh Kumaiya, Askoti, Soryali, Sirali, Chaugarkhyali, Gangola, Kumaiya, Khasparjia, Pachhai, Phaldakoti, And Rauchaubhaisi. All These Mentioned Dialects Of Garhwali And Kumaoni Are Jointly Known As Central Pahari Group Of Languages. Khaskura (Nepali) Is Spoken In The East Of Kumaon Region, Western Pahari (Himachali) In The West, Tibeto - Burmese Family In The Noth And Western Hindi In The South.

Kumaon Contains Extremely Wealthy Tradition Of Folk Literature, Which Deals With Heroes, Local/National Myths, Heroines, Several Aspects Of Nature And Deeds Of Bravery. Anonymous Poets Wrote These Songs Which Related To The Deeds Of Gods-Goddesses, Creation Of Earth, Local Heroes/ Dynasties And Several Characters Belong To Mahabharat And Ramayan. Some Of Those Songs Are Also Associated With Exceptional Love Story Of Rajula And Malushahi, The Heroism Of Sangram Singh Karki, The Daring Deeds Of The Twenty Two Bafaul Brothers And The Unreal Terrains Across The Himalaya. These Songs Are Sung By Experts By Considering The Local History And Bharau. You Can Experience These Songs On Agricultural Activities And Diverse Cultural And Social Festivals.

Other Varieties Of Songs Are Agricultural, Pastoral And Children's Songs That Shows The Sealed Relationship Between Man And His Surrounds. These Songs Also Describe The Natural Beauty Of This Region That Is Really Exceptional. Varieties Of Folk Songs Such As The Invitation Songs, Bhagnaul, Neoli, Chanchari, Jhora And Chhapeli. You Will Find The Word 'Suva' Or P'arrot That Denotes Lovers, Whereas In The 'Riturain' Songs, The 'Nyoli' Bird Denotes Bothers And Sisters. Neoli Is Also Acknowledged As The Style Of Singing. Some Of The Well-Known Singers Of Kumain District Are Mohan Singh Reethagari, Gopidas, Chakra Ram Damai And Jait Ram.

If You Talk About The Written Literature Of Kumaon Then The Most Famous Names Are Krishna Pandey, Lok Ratna Pant 'Gumani', Shiv Datt Sati, Shyama Charan Datt Pant, Gorda, Ram Dutt Pant 'Kaviraj', Pitambar Pandey, Chandra Lal Chaudhary, Bachi Ram Arya, Kunwar Singh Bhandari, Jeevan Chandra Joshi, Etc. Nowadays, Writers And Poets Of Kumaon Are Not Only Famous Inside Kumaon Region But Also Outside The Kumaon. They Gave Their Exceptional Contribution To Hindi Literature And Journalism. Amongst The Crowd, Contribution Of Sumitra Nandan Pant, Gumani, Laxmi Datt Joshi, Ela Chandra Joshi, Shailesh Matiyani, Hem Chandra Joshi, Pankaj Bisht And Mrinal Pande Are Broadly Accepted.

The Shauka, Tharu, Banraji And Boksa Tribes Are Also Known For Their Outstanding Folk Songs And Dances. You Can Experience These Songs And Dances During Social Cultural Ceremonies And Festivals. Talking About The Extremely Famous Dance Of Kumaon, The Chhalaria, Or Chholia Always Takes The Lead Position Amongst The Availability. These Dance Forms Are Associated With The Martial Tradition Of The Region. View Of The Bhagnaul, Jhora And Chanchari Along With Famous Dance Form Of Uttarakhand Is Always Outstanding. Nowadays, You Can Experience These Songs During Fairs And Festivals.

5

Geography and Flora & Fauna

GEOGRAPHY OF UTTARAKHAND

Uttarakhand has a total geographic area of 53,483 km^2, of which 86% is mountainous and 65% is covered by forest.

Nanda Devi is the highest mountain of Uttarakhand and second-highest mountain in India.

Valley of Flowers

Most of the northern parts of the state are part of Greater Himalaya ranges, covered by the high Himalayan peaks and glaciers, while the lower foothills were densely forested till denuded by the British log merchants and later, after independence, by forest contractors.

A panorama of Garhwal Himalaya from Dhanaulti

Recent efforts in reforestation, however, have been successful in restoring the situation to some extent. The unique Himalayan ecosystem plays host to a large number of animals (including bharal, snow leopards, leopards and tigers), plants and rare herbs. Two of India's mighties, the Ganges and the Yamuna take birth in the glaciers of Uttarakhand, and are fed by myriad lakes, glacial melts and streams.

Geography

With the elevation of 7,816 metres (25,643 ft) above sea level, Nanda Devi is the highest mountain in Uttarakhand and the second-highest mountain in India, following Kangchenjunga in Sikkim.

Uttarakhand has a total area of 53,483 km, of which 86% is mountainous and 65% is covered by forest. Most of the northern part of the state is covered by high Himalayan peaks and glaciers. In the first half of the nineteenth century, the expanding development of Indian roads, railways and other physical infrastructure was giving rise to concerns over indiscriminate logging, particularly in the Himalaya. Two of the most important rivers in Hinduism originate in the glaciers of Uttarakhand, the Ganges at Gangotri and the Yamuna at Yamunotri. They are fed by myriad lakes, glacial melts and streams. These two along with Badrinath and Kedarnath form the Chota Char Dham, a holy pilgrimage for the Hindus.

The state hosts the Bengal tiger in Jim Corbett National

Park, the oldest national park of the Indian subcontinent. The Valley of Flowers, a UNESCO World Heritage Site located in the upper expanses of Bhyundar Ganga near Joshimath in Gharwal region, is known for the variety and rarity of its flowers and plants. One who raised this was Sir Joseph Dalton Hooker, Director of the Royal Botanic Gardens, Kew, who visited the region. As a consequence, Lord Dalhousie issued the Indian Forest Charter in 1855, reversing the previous laissez-faire policy. The following Indian Forest Act of 1878 put Indian forestry on a solid scientific basis. A direct consequence was the founding of the Imperial Forest School at Dehradun by Dietrich Brandis in 1878. Renamed the 'Imperial Forest Research Institute' in 1906, it is now known as the Forest Research Institute (India).

The model "Forest Circles" around Dehradun, used for training, demonstration and scientific measurements, had a lasting positive influence on the forests and ecology of the region. The Himalayan ecosystem provides habitat for many animals (including bharal, snow leopards, leopards and tigers), plants, and rare herbs.

Uttarakhand lies on the southern slope of the Himalaya range, and the climate and vegetation vary greatly with elevation, from glaciers at the highest elevations to subtropical forests at the lower elevations. The highest elevations are covered by ice and bare rock. Below them, between 3,000 and 5,000 metres (9,800 and 16,400 ft) are the western Himalayan alpine shrub and meadows. The temperate western Himalayan subalpine conifer forestsgrow just below the tree line. At 3,000 to 2,600 metres (9,800 to 8,500 ft) elevation they transition to the temperate western Himalayan broadleaf forests, which lie in a belt from 2,600 to 1,500 metres (8,500 to 4,900 ft) elevation. Below 1,500 metres (4,900 ft) elevation lie the Himalayan subtropical pine forests. The Upper Gangetic Plains moist deciduous forests and the drier Terai-Duar savanna and grasslands cover the lowlands along the Uttar Pradesh border in a belt locally known as Bhabar. These lowland forests have mostly been cleared for agriculture, but a few pockets remain.

In June 2013 several days of extremely heavy rain caused

devastating floods in the region, resulting in more than 5000 people missing and presumed dead. The flooding was referred to in the Indian media as a "Himalayan Tsunami".

Terrain and vegetation

Uttarakhand lies on the south slope of the Himalaya range, and the climate and vegetation vary greatly with elevation, from glaciers at the highest elevations to tropical forests at the lower elevations. The highest elevations are covered by ice and bare rock. Mount Nanda Devi is the highest peak of Uttarakhand with the altitude of 7816 m above sea level. Western Himalayan alpine shrub and meadows occur between 3,000 and 5,000 metres (9,800 and 16,400 ft): tundra and alpine meadows cover the highest elevations, *Rhododendron*-dominated shrublands cover the lower elevations. Western Himalayan subalpine conifer forests lie just below the tree line; at 3,000 to 2,600 metres (9,800 to 8,500 ft) elevation they transition to western Himalayan broadleaf forests, which lie in a belt from 2,600 to 1,500 metres (8,500 to 4,900 ft) elevation. Below 1,500 metres (4,900 ft) elevation lie the Himalayan subtropical pine forests. The drier Terai-Duar savanna and grasslands belt and the Upper Gangetic Plains moist deciduous forests cover the lowlands along the Uttar Pradesh border. This belt is locally known as Bhabar. These lowland forests have mostly been cleared for agriculture, but a few pockets remain.

National parks

Indian National Parks in Uttarakhand include the Jim Corbett National Park previously named as Hailey National Park (the oldest national park of India) in Nainital District and Pauri Garhwal District, Valley of Flowers National Park & Nanda Devi National Park in Chamoli District, which together are a UNESCO World Heritage Site, Rajaji National Park in Haridwar District and Dehradun District and Govind Pashu Vihar National Park & Gangotri National Park in Uttarkashi District.

STATISTICS

- *Total Geographical Area*: 51,125 km²
  Hill Area: 92.57%
  Plain Area: 7.43%
  Area Covered By Forest: 63%
- *Location*
  Longitude 77° 34' 27" East to 81° 02' 22" E
  Latitude 28° 53' 24" North to 31° 27' 50" N
- *Total Population*: 7,050,634 (Male : Female = 1000 : 976)
  Male: % 51.91
  Female: % 48.81
  Rural Population: 76.90%
  Urban Population: 23.10%
  Other Minorities: 2.0% (approx)
- *Primary Ethnic Group*: Indo-Aryans
- *Literacy Rate*: 72%
- *Villages*: 15620
- *Cities and Urban Areas*: 81
- *Railway Stations*: Kotdwar, Dehradun, Haridwar, Rishikesh, Haldwani, Lalkuan, Kathgodam, Ramnagar, Tanakpur
- *Airports*: Jolly Grant, Pantnagar, Nainisain, Gauchar (Helipad)
- *Major Peaks* (height in metres above sea level) : Nanda Devi (7816), Kamet (7756), Badrinath (7140), Chaukhamba (7138), Trishul (7120), Dunagiri (7066), Panch Chhuli (6910), Nanda Kot (6861), Gangotri (6614), Gauri Parvat (6590)
- *Major Passes* : Mana La (5450), Niti La (5070), Lipu Lekh La (5122), Lumpia Dhura (5650)
- *Industry* : Tourism, Hydroelectricity Production, Dairy, Agriculture, Horticulture, Floriculture, Sugar, Manufacturing, and other small scale industries

- *Festivals :* Uttarani, Nanda Devi Mela, Holi, Diwali, Dasara, Kandali, Hilljatra, Bikhoti, Bagwal, Harela, Ghugutee
- *Events :* Sardotsav, Basantotsav, Nanda Devi Raj Jat, Chipla Kedar Jaat, Kedarnath Yatra, Badrinath Yatra, Kumbh Mela, Ardh Kumbh Mela, Ramleela, Uttarakhand Mahotsav (Dehradun)
- *Trade Centres :* Haldwani, Rudrapur, Roorkee, Tanakpur, Dehradun, Haridwar, Kotdwar, Rishikesh

DISTRICTS OF UTTARAKHAND

Uttarakhand is divided into 13 districts: Almora, Bageshwar, Chamoli, Champawat, Dehradun, Haridwar, Nainital, Pauri (Pauri Garhwal), Pithoragarh, Rudraprayag, Tehri (Tehri Garhwal), Udham Singh Nagar, and Uttarkashi. These districts form two divisions; Garhwal division includes Chamoli, Dehradun, Haridwar, Pauri Garhwal, Rudraprayag, Tehri, and Uttarkashi districts, and Kumaon division includes Almora, Bageshwar, Champawat, Nainital, Pithoragarh, and Udham Singh Nagar.

A district of Uttarakhand state is an administrative geographical unit, headed by a Deputy Commissioner or District Magistrate, an officer belonging to the Indian Administrative Service. The district magistrate or the deputy commissioner is assisted by a number of officers belonging to Uttarakhand Civil Service and other Uttarakhand state services.

A Superintendent of Police, an officer belonging to the Indian Police Service is entrusted with the responsibility of maintaining law and order and related issues of the district. He is assisted by the officers of the Uttarakhand Police Service and other Uttarakhand Police officials.

A Deputy Conservator of Forests, an officer belonging to the Indian Forest Service is responsible for managing the Forests, environment and wildlife related issues of the district. He is assisted by the officers of the Uttarakhand Forest Service and other Uttarakhand Forest officials and Uttarakhand Wild-Life officials.

Sectoral development is looked after by the district head of each development department such as PWD, Health, Education, Agriculture, Animal husbandry, etc. These officers belong to the various State Services.

State	*Code*	*District*	*Headquarters*	*Population 2001*	*Area (km²)*	*Density (km²)*
UT	AL	Almora	Almora	630446	3090	204
UT	BA	Bageshwar	Bageshwar	249453	2310	108
UT	CL	Chamoli	Chamoli	369198	7692	48
UT	CP	Champawat	Champawat	224461	1781	126
UT	DD	Dehradun	Dehradun	1279083	3088	414
UT	HA	Haridwar	Haridwar	1444213	2360	612

Contd...

State.	*Code*	*District*	*Headquarters*	*Population 2001*	*Area (km²)*	*Density (km²)*
UT	NA	Nainital	Nainital	762912	3853	198
UT	PG	Pauri Garhwal	Pauri	696851	5438	128
UT	PI	Pithoragarh	Pithoragarh	462149	7110	65
UT	RP	Rudra Prayag	Rudraprayag	227461	1896	120
UT	TG	Tehri Garhwal	New Tehri	604608	4085	148
UT	US	Udham Singh Nagar	Rudrapur	1234548	2912	424
UT	UT	Uttarkashi	Uttarkashi	294179	7951	37

Almora

Almora is a district of Uttarakhand state, India. The headquarters is at Almora. Almora is a picturesque district in the Kumaon division of Uttarakhand in India. It has a panoramic view of the Himalayas. Tourists from all over the world come to see the natural beauty of the district. Almora is famous for its cultural heritage, handicrafts, cuisine and wildlife.

History: The ancient town of Almora, before its establishment was under the possession of Katyuri king Baichaldeo. He donated major part of this land to a Gujrati Brahmin Sri Chand Tiwari. Later on when Chand kingdom was founded in Baramandal, the town of Almora was founded at this centrally located place in 1560 by Kalyan Chand. In the days of the Chand Kings it was called Rajapur. The name

'Rajpur' is also mentioned over a number of ancient copper plates.

Geography: The town of Almora is situated over a horse saddle shaped ridge of a mountain. The eastern portion of the ridge is known as Talifat and the western one is known as Selifat. The market is at the top of the ridge where these two, Talifat and Selifat jointly terminate.

The market is 1.25 miles long and is covered with stone slabs. The place of the present cantonment was formerly known as Lalmandi. Presently where the collectorate exists, the 'Malla Mahal' (Upper Court) of Chanda kings was located. The site of present District Hospital used to be 'Talla Mahal' (Lower Court) of Chand rulers. Simalkhet is a village situated in the border of Almora and Chamoli. People of this village can speak both kumauni and garhwali languages. On the top of a hill there is a temple called bhairav gadi. This temple is very famous in the region.

Gori River flows through Almora District: Almora was also the site of the famous dance academy set up by Udai Shankar, the famous danseuse in the 1938 - several famous Indian and French dancers trained here. The Almora dance academy was housed in Pine Lodge on the outskirts of the town (Ranidhara). The site has a fantastic views of the Himalayas and the city.

"In these hills, nature's hospitality eclipses all men can ever do. The enchanting beauties of the Himalayas, their bracing climate and the soothing green that envelopes you leaves nothing more to be desired. I wonder whether the scenery of these hills and the climate are to be surpassed, if equalled, by any of the beauty spots of the world. After having been nearly three weeks in Almora Hills, I am more than ever amazed why our people need go in Europe in search of health." - Mahatma M.K. Gandhi

"These mountains are associated with the best memories of our race: Here, therefore, must be one of centres, not merely of activity, but more of calmness of meditation, and of peace and I hope some one to realize it." - Swami Vivekananda (replying to the address given to him by the people of Almora).

Transport

Air: Nearest Airport is Pantnagar (Nainital): 127 km.

Train: Nearest Railway Station is at Kathgodam, 90 km, from where direct trains are available for Delhi, Lucknow and Agra. Some of the important trains for Kathgodam are:

- Shatabdi Express
- Howrah Express (3019/3020)
- Ranikhet Express (5013/5014)
- Rampur Passenger (1/2 R.K. Passenger and 3/4 R.K. Passenger)
- Nainital Express (5308/5307)

Road: Almora is well connected by road to important centres in the region. Some distances:

- Delhi (378 km)
- Lucknow (460 km)
- Nainital (66 km) (via Ranikhet 103 km)
- Kathgodam (90 km)

Bageshwar

Bageshwar District is a district of Uttarakhand state in northern India. The town of Bageshwar is the district headquarters. Bageshwar District is in the eastern Kumaon region of Uttarakhand, and is bounded on the west and northwest by Chamoli District, on the northeast and east by Pithoragarh District, and on the south by Almora District.

Chamoli

Chamoli is a district of Uttarakhand state of India. It is bounded by the Tibet region of China to the north, and by the Uttarakhand districts of Pithoragarh and Bageshwar to the east, Almora to the south, Garhwal to the southwest, Rudraprayag to the west, and Uttarkashi to the northwest. The administrative headquarters of the district is Gopeshwar. The district is largely inhabited by Tibetans of the Bhotiya ethnic group who adhere to Hinduism.

Champawat

Champawat District is a district of Uttarakhand state in northern India. The town of Champawat is the administrative headquarters.

Champawat District is part of the eastern Kumaon Division of Uttarakhand. It is bounded on the north by Pithoragarh District, on the east by Nepal, on the south by Udham Singh Nagar District, on the west by Nainital District, and on the northwest by Almora District

Dehradun

Dehradun pronunciations a district of Uttarakhand state in northern India. The district headquarters is Dehradun, which has also served as the provisional capital of Uttarakhand since its founding in 2000, and may well become the permanent capital. The region was seized as a war spoil from the Maharaja of Tehri-Garhwal as a consequence of the Gurkha War of 1814-16, and attached administratively to Saharanpur District to its immediate south, which was already in British hands.

Dehradun District also includes the prominent towns of Rishikesh, Mussoorie, Landour and Chakrata. The district stretches from the Ganges river in the east to the Yamuna river in the west, and from the Terai and Shivaliks in the south and southeast to the Great Himalaya in the northwest.

Garhwal

Garhwal District is a former district of British India and later of the Indian state of Uttar Pradesh, it has been divided into the present-day districts of Chamoli, Pauri Garhwal, and Rudraprayag.

Haridwar

Haridwar pronunciations a district of Uttarakhand state,

India. The headquarter is at Haridwar. Another town in the district is Roorkee.

Nainital

Nainital is a district of Uttarakhand state, India. The headquarter is at Nainital. Nainital District is located in Kumaon Division, and is bounded on the north by the Almora District and on the south by the Udham Singh Nagar District. Haldwani is the largest town in the district.

Pauri

Pauri Garhwal is a district of Uttarakhand state, India. The headquarter is at Pauri. Diverse in topography, the district of Pauri Garhwal varies from the foothills of the Tarai of Kotdwar to Srinagar valley, Landsdowne & the soul- lifting meadows of Doonhatoli, sprawing at an altitude of 3,000mts., which remain snowbound during the winter months. Pauri Garhwal is ringed by the districts of Chamoli, Nainital, Haridwar, Dehradun, Rudraprayag and Tehri Garhwal. Filled with places of tourist interest, most locations in Pauri offer a breathtaking view of the snow - laden Himalayan splendour.

It is situated at an elevation of 1814 meters above sea-level on the northern slopes of the Kandoliya hills. Pauri is the headquarters of the district Pauri Garhwal and the Garhwal Division. Pauri provides a panoramic view of the Himalayan peaks of Bandar Poonch, Swarga-Rohini, Jonli, the Gangotri Group, the Jogin Group, Thalaiya-sagar, Kedarnath, Kharcha Kund, Sumeru, Satopanth, Chaukhamba, Neelkanth, Ghoriparvat, Hathiparvat, Nandadevi and Trisul.

- *Area* : 5 km^2.
- *Population* : 20,397 (1991 census)
- *Altitude* : 1,814 mts.
- *Climate* : Cold in winter, pleasant in summer and heavy rainfall in monsoon.
- *Season* : Round the year.
- *Clothing: Summer* : Cottons/ light woollens,

- *Winter* : Heavy Woollens
- *Languages* : Garhwali, Hindi & English.

Shopping Centres

- Upper Bazar
- Lower Bazar
- Dhara Road

Pilgrimage: Siddhibali Temple, Durga Devi Temple, Medanpuri Devi Temple, Shri Koteshwar Mahadev Tarkeshwar Mahadev, Keshorai Math, Kamleshwar Temple, Shankar Math, Devalgarh Dhar Devi, Kinkaleshwar Mandir, Kandoliya Mandir.

Khirsu: The snow-covered mountains of Khirsu offers a panoramic view of the Central Himalayas and attracts a large number of tourists. From here one can get a clear view of many named & unnamed peaks.

Located 19 km. away from Pauri at an altitude of 1,700 mts., Khirsu is a peaceful spot, free from pollution. The tranquillity of the adjoining thick Oak and Deodar forests and apple orchards, is broken only by the chirping of birds. The ancient temple of Ghandiyal Devta in the vicinity is well worth a visit. Accommodation is available at the Tourist Rest House and Forest Rest House.

Doodhatoli: Doodhatoli, situated at an altitude of 3100 mts., is covered with dense mixed forests. Thalisain is the last bus terminus (100 km. from Pauri), from where Doodhatoli is at a distance of 24 km. by trek. One of the most pictureque places, it commands a panoramic view of the Himalayan ranges and the surrounding area.

The indometable freedom fighter of Garhwal, Veer Chandra Singh Garwali, was enamoured by the place. As was his last wish, a memorial in his name has been erected here after his death. A humble but bold memorial in his name creates a 'never say die' atmosphere under the tall Oak trees.

Jwalpa-Devi-Temple: It is one of the well known religious places of the entire division and a large number of devotees come here round the year for darshan. It is 34 km. from Pauri on the main Pauri-Kotdwar road. Every year during 'Navaratras', a special religious festival is held at Jwaladevi.

Binsar Mahadev: Binsar is situated at an altitude of 2480 mts. and is at a distance of 114 km. from Pauri. Set amidst dense forest of Oak, Deodar and Rhododendron, it is a celebrated place of worship. The temple dedicated to Lord Shiva is of archaeological significance. The central room of the temple is beautifully adorned by the idols of Ganesh, Har Gauri and Mardini. Thalisain, 100 km. from Pauri, is the last bus stop. From here a 22 km. bridle path leads to Binsar. Camp in luxury at The Binsar Retreat.

Adwani: Connected by a well maintained 17 km. long road from Pauri, Adwani is an ideal picnic spot, as it is surrounded by thick forest and devoid of the hustle & bustle of the town. There is a Forest Rest House one can stay. Adwani is one of bus stand for near villages like khaproli, nagoli, bangaonmalla.. etc.. many villages are near its boundary. Cheed, banj, kafal, bhnwara, burash and many more trees and fruits are found in this jungle.

Tarakund: Situated at a height of 2,200 mts., Tara Kund is a picturesque spot amidst lofty mountains in the Chariserh development area. A small lake and an ancient temple adorn the place. The Teej Festival is celebrated with great gaiety when the local people come here to worship and pay homage to God.

Kanvashram: Situated at a distance of 14 km. from Kotdwar, Kanva Rishi Ashram is an important place from the historical and archaeological point of view. It is believed that Sage Vishwamitra meditated here. Indra, the king of Gods, was scared by his intense meditation, and sent a beautiful heavenly damsel named Menka to disturb him. Menka finally succeeded in diverting Vishwamitra's attention. After birth to a girl she went back to heaven. The girl later became Shakuntala who got married to the prince of Hastinapur and gave birth to Bharat, the prince after whom our country is called Bharat. Accommodation is available at tourist complex, Kanvashram.

Bharat Nagar: 22 km. away from Kotdwar and at a height of 1,400 mts., Bharatnagar abounds in immense natural beauty. It is mentioned in the ancient Hindu texts that once this place was full of life giving herbs. From here one can have a beautiful view of the Balawali bridge on Ganga, Kalagarh dam and Kotdwar.

Neelkanth: Just 32 km. from Rishikesh via Barrage and 22 km. via Ram Jhoola, this place abounds in religious fervour, mythological significance and picturesque surroundings. According to a legend, this place derived its name from Lord Shiva. It is believed that it was here that Lord Shiva consumed the venom which emanated durimg the ' Samudra Manthan ' due to this, His throat became blue in colour, thus giving Shiva the name of Neelkanth. Centuries old temples here reserve in their fold the celestial aura and legendary ambience.

At 926 meters, amidst three valleys (vishnukoot, Brahmakoot and Manikoot) and on the confluence of Madhumati and Pankaja rivers awaits Neelkanth mahadev. Neelkanth Mahadev is 22 km. from Swargashram. The 12 km. trekkable road is surrounded by dense forests, a sight every trekker would love to behold.

Chila: Chila Wildlife Sanctuary, a heaven for animal watchers, is just 8 km. from Haridwar and 21 km from Rishikesh. Located on the banks of river Ganga in the heart of Shivalik hills, Chila is a part of the famous Rajaji National Park. The fauna include elephants, spotted Deer, Stag deer, Neelgai bull, Wild beer, Fox, Porcupine, Jungle fowls and Peacocks. Beside these, migratory birds are also seen on the river Ganga. There is a Tourist Rest House in addition to a Forest Rest House.

Kalagarh: Situated at a distance of 48 km. from Kotdwar, Kalagarh is an ideal places for nature lovers. The dam across Ram Ganga river is also worth visiting. Accommodation is available at the irrigation & Forest Rest Houses.

Lwali: Situated at a distance of 4 km. from Pauri, and 3 km. from Kandoliya is a quick trip to see the inner working of typical Garwali life at work. Lwali is a small valley town of

20-30 shops and 15-20 houses. It is situated around the Madhyamik Vidyalaya (Middle School) Lwali.

Accessibility

Air : Nearest airport is Jollygrant (155 km.) via Rishikesh - Srinagar Rail : Nearest railway station is Kotdwar (108 km.) Road : Pauri is well connected to Dehradun, Rishikesh, Kotdwar and other cities of the region.

Pithoragarh

Pithoragarh is the easternmost Himalayan district in the state of Uttarakhand, India. It is naturally landscaped with high Himalayan mountains, snow capped peaks, passes, valleys, alpine meadows, forests, waterfalls, perennial rivers, glaciers and springs. The flora and fauna of this area has rich ecological diversity. The geographical area of the district is 7169 km^2. As per the 2001 census, the total population of the district is 4,62,149.

The total literacy rate is 76.48 percent. Pithoragarh town, which is located in Sour or Saur valley is also its headquarter. The district is the part of Kumaon region of Uttarakhand state and which is also one of its administrative division. Pithoragarh has many temples and ruined forts reminiscent of the once flourising reign of Chand Kings. There is Tibet plateau situated to the north of the district. Nepal lies on the eastern borders. The River Kali originates from Kalapaani, forms its continuous eastern boundary with Nepal. It is an Indian border district with China. The Hindu pilgrimage route for Mount Kailash-Lake Mansarovar passes through this district via Lipu-Lekh pass in the greater Himalayas. Previously, it was the part of Almora district of Uttarakhand, but, in 1960, Pithoragarh, as a separate district, was created.

In 1997 a new district of Champawat was formed out of it, by reorganizing its boundaries. The district is administratively divided into five tehsils, namely Munsiyari, Dharchula, Didihat, Gangolihat, and Pithoragarh. Naini Saini is the nearest civil airport. The mineral deposits present in the district are magnesium ore, copper ore, limestones and slate stone.

Origin of the Name: During the reign of King Bharati chand (1437-1450) of Chand dynasty, his son Ratna Chand defeated Doti Kinga Of Nepal and captured Soar or Saur valley and annexed it to Kumaon or Kurmanchal in 1449. During his reign Peeru Or Prithivi Gussain Built a fort on his name called 'Pithora Garh' in Soar valley, later this place came to be known as Pithoragarh, after the name of the fort.

Brief History—Language: The widely spoken language is Kumauni with its numerous variations. Kumaoni is a dialect written in Devanagari script. Bhotiya tribe speak Tibetan mix dialect called 'Beyansi' or 'Bhotia' or 'Hunia', which is the language of Tibeto-Burman family. Van Rawat tribe speak their own Kumaoni variant.

Climate: Pithoragarh town, being in the valley, is relatively warm during summer and cool during winters. During the coldest months of December - January, the tropical and temperate mountain ridges and high locations receive snowfall and has an average monthly temperature ranging between 5.5°C and 8°C. Pithoragarh district have extreme variation in temperature due to much altitude gradient. The temperature starts rising from mid March till mid June. The areas situated above 3,500 m remain in a permanent snow cover. Regions lying between 3,000 to 3,500 m become snow bound for four to six months. There are extreme points present at the different places like river gorges at Dharchula, Jhulaghat, Ghat and Sera, where sometimes temperature rises up to 40°C.

The annual average rainfall is 36.7 cm. After June the district receives Monsoon showers. Winter set for transhumance - seasonal migration among the Bhotiya tribe with their herds of livestocks to lower warmer areas. & any problms say Kishor Bhatt.

Seasons

- Winter or Cold weather (December - March)

- Summer or hot weather (March - June)
- Season of general rains (North - West monsoon-Mid June to mid September)
- Season of retreating monsoon (September to November)

Native Tribes: Tribes inhabiting in the district are Van Rawats and Bhotiya. Both the tribes are nomadic; Van Rawats are hunter-gatherers too. Bhotiyas are basically sheep and goat reare and traders of Tibet. Bhotiya tribe celebrates Kandali Festival and organize country clubs called 'Rang Bhang'.

Glaciers of Pithoragarh: Locally glaciers are known as Gal. Some important glaciers of the districts are as follows: Milam Glacier, Namik Glacier, Ralam Glacier, Meola Glacier, Sona Glacier, Panchchuli Glacier, Balati Glacier, Shipu Glacier, Rula Glacier, Kalabaland Glacier, Lawan Glacier, Bamlas Glacier, Baldimga Glacier, Terahar Glacier, Poting Glacier, Talkot Glacier, Sankalpa, Lassar Glacier, Dhauli Glacier, Baling Golfu Glacier, Dhauli Glacier, Sobla Tejam Glacier, Kali Glacier, Kuti Glacier, Yangti Basin Glacier.

Himalayan Peaks of Pithoragarh: Peaks 7,000 M and over

Nanda Devi East-7434 M, Hardeol-7,151 M, Trishuli-7,074 M.

Peaks 6,000 M and Over

Rishi Pahar-6,992 M; Nanda Kot-6,861 M; Chiring We-6,559 M; Rajrambha-6,537 M; Chaudhara-6,510 M; Sangthang-6,480 M; Panchchuli-6,437 M; Nagalaphu-6,410 M; Suitilla (Suj Tilla West)-6,374 M; Suj Tilla East-6,393 M; Bamba Dhura-6,334 M; Burphu Dhura-6,334 M; Changuch-6,322 M; Nanda Gond-6,315 M; Nanda Pal-6,306 M; Suli Top-6,300 M; Kuchela-6,294 M; Nital Thaur-6,236 M; Kalganga Dhura-6,215 M; Jonglingkong or Baba Kailash - 6,191 M; Lalla We-6,123 M; Kalabaland Dhura-6,105 M; Telkot-6,102 M; Bainti-6,079 M; Ikualari-6,059 M; Nagling-6,041 M; Menaka Peak-6,000 M;

Peaks 5,000 M and Over

Trigal-5,983 M; Yungtangto-5,945 M; Sankalp-5,929 M; Laspa Dhura-5,913 M; Sahdev-5,782 M; Ralam Dhura-5,630 M; Gilding Peak-5,629 M; Shivu-5,255 M; Tihutia-5,252 M; Draupadi Peak-5,250 M; Rambha Kot-5,221 M; Panchali Chuli-5,220 M.

Mountain Passes of Pithoragarh

International Passes to Tibet: Lampiya Dhura- (5,530 m); Lipu-Lekh pass - (5,450 m); Lowe Dhura- (5,562 m); Mangshya Dhura- (5,630 m); Nuwe Dhura- (5,650 m).

Intra District Himalayan Passes: Kungri Bhingri La- (5,564 M); Nama pass- (5,500 M); Sinla pass- (5,495 M); Ralam pass- (5,630 M); Keo Dhura- (5,439 M); Belcha Dhura- (5,384 M); Kalganga Dhura-(5,312 M); Traills pass- (5,312 M); Gangchal Dhura- (5,050 M); Bircjrang Dhura (4,666 M); Ghatmila Dhura; Unta Dhura pass; Yangkchar Dhura- (4,800 M); Rur Khan- (3,800 M); Bainti Col- (5,100 M); Longstaff Col- (5,910 M).

Valleys of Pithoragarh: Daramaganga or Darma valley, Goriganga valley, Kali valley, Kuthi valley, Lassar Yangti valley, Ralam valley, Kuthi Yangti valley, Milam or Johar valley, Kalabaland valley, Byans valley, Chaudans valley, Saur valley

Waterfalls of Pithoragarh: Lim Bagudiyar Fall, Birthi Fall, Pilsitti Fall, Garaun Fall

Flora: Flora includes many unique sub-tropical, temperate and alpine plants. The flora of the district includes many Bryophytes, Pteridophytes, Gymnosperms and Angiosperms. Rare varieties of Orchids are also present in the high altitude valleys of Milan, Darma, Beyans and Kuthi. Among them Myrica esculenta (Kafal), Saussurea obvallata (Brahm Kamal), Zanthoxylem armatum (Timur), Berberis aristata (Kirmod), Saussurea simpsonia, Rhododendron campanulatum, Rubus rotundifolius (Hisalu) Rhododendron barbatum (Burans), Cypripedium cordigerum, Dendrobium normale, Vanda cristata, Prunus puddum, Prunus cornuta, Pedicularis punctata, Quercus incana, Quercus leucotricophora (Banjh), Quercus semicarpifolia,

Quercus dilatata, Pinus roxburghii (Salla or Chir), Pinus wallichiana (Blue Pine or Raisalla), Cedrus deodara (Deodar Cedar), Taxus wallichiana (Himalayan yew), Abies pindrow, Aconitum heterophyllum, Betula utilis (Himalayan birch or Bhoj Patra), Nardostachys grandiflora (Jatmasi), Picorrhiza kurroa (Kutki).

FAUNA AND FLORA OF UTTARAKHAND

Uttarakhand is endowed with a unique and diverse range of biodiversity. From the snowbound peaks of the Himalayas to the moist Alpine scrub, sub Alpine forests, dry - temperate and moist-temperate forests to moist deciduous forests, the state possesses a wide biodiversity that in return nurtures a large multiplicity of floral and faunal forms.

The state is home to nearly 4048 species of Angiosperms and Gymnosperms belonging to 1198 genera under 192 families. Of these nearly 116 species are specific to Uttarakhand i.e. their geographical distribution is limited to the boundaries of the state. 161 species of flora found in Uttarakhand are recognized as rare or threatened under the categorization of the International Union for Conservation of Nature (IUCN). Out of the 223 species of Orchids reported from the North Western Himalayas, over 150 have been reported from the State.

This great floral diversity supports a wide variety of faunal forms too. It includes about 102 species of mammals, 623 species of birds, 124 species of fish, 69 species of reptiles and 19 species of amphibians. Highly endangered species like the Snow Leopard, Musk Deer, Tiger, Asian Elephant, Bharal, Himalayan Monal, Cheer Pheasant, King Cobra etc. find suitable habitat in the forests of Uttarakhand.

This precious natural wealth is our common heritage. In order to conserve this heritage, the state has declared twelve areas as 'Protected' including 6 National Parks and six Wildlife Sanctuaries. Nearly 65% of the geographical area of the State is under forest cover, of which over 12% comes under the Protected Area network. This exceeds the national average by a fair margin and is a reflection of the state's commitment to conservation. The Corbett National Park, established in 1936 is the first National Park of the Asian mainland. The Nandadevi Biosphere Reserve, established under the "Man and biosphere" programme of UNESCO has the honour of being Uttarakhand's only and the country's second Biosphere Reserve. This biodiversity wealth is the pride of Uttarakhand.

Fauna

Uttarakhand is home to may species of deer – the magnificent Sambar with heavy antlers, which is called Jarau in the hills, the beautiful Chital, the rare Barasinga or swamp deer, the Kasturi or musk deer, so named because the buck has a gland beneath the skin of the abdomen that secretes musk, the Kakar, rib-faced or barking deer which is a very pretty little animal, bright chestnut in colour with forked horns, and many others.

Other interesting animals are the Goral of the antelope family also known as the Himalayan Chamois, the Bharal or wild blue sheep, the Ibex, a handsome animal and usually greyish in colour but now rarely seen in the Uttarakhand mountains, the brown and black bears, the agile Himalayan Thar, the Himalayan Fox, a fine beast with a thick coat of fur, indigenous sheep etc. With these, there also are the killers, the Himalayan leopard and tiger who are being squeezed into the diminishing forests. The foothills near Haridwar, Kotdwara, Ramnagar, Dhikala have large herds of elephants , some of them easy to observe in the Corbet national Park and Rajaji Park. And if one is lucky, the tigers of Corbet fame may be sighted as a matter of chance.

Flowers and trees

The flowers, shrubs and trees are wide in variety, colourful and fragrant in this land of Uttarakhand – blue poppies, pink and purple primulas, asters, potentilas of many colour, varied alpine flowers, the heavily perfumed brahma kamal, rhododendrons with large ruby-red flowers, fragrant white syringa, cotoneaster with its red berries, sweet jasmine, lillies of different kinds, acacia, cypresses, pines, oaks, deodars, firs, spruces etc.

Medicinal and aromatic plants – Junipers, Digitalis Purpurea (fox glove), its leaves are used in curing heart disease, Gentiana (gentian), the flowers are purple, intense blue, white and yellow (root of which is used in medicine to stimulate digestion); Pyrethrum (feverfew) has aromatic yellow leaves which are used in insecticides, Seasamum Indicum (sesame) has small oily seeds which yield a tasteless oil used in cooking and some cosmetics, Mentha Viridis (spearmint) the oil obtained by distillation from the fresh herb in flower is good in cases of cholic, nausea etc. (this para is here with the help of some botanist friend).

Birds

Birds, birds and birds of Uttarakhand and indeed there are many – Cuckoos, Himalayan Magpies, Kingfishers, Orioles, white-capped Redstarts, Robins, Shrikes, Swallows, Swifts, Thrushes, Tree Creepers, Yellow and pied Wagtails, Warblers, Water Ouzels, Woodpeckers, black drongo and many more.

The Munal, an exotic pheasant with brilliant plumage, which has been adjudged as the "Bird of the state" by Uttarakhand, is found at above 2439 mtr to 3658 mtr. The well-known Chakor is very common among the partridges, and in the extreme north, the raucous note of the black partridge is often heard.

The Himalayan Snow Cock is found on or about the snow-line. Amongst Pigeons, the blue rock and the wood Pigeon are very common. Birds of prey such as Eagles, Falcons, Hawks and Vultures are frequently seen.

Bird watching

Around the lakes, bird watching is good, especially Naukuchiatal (27 km from Nainital), Asan Barrage (32 kms from Dehradun) and Dodital (32 km trek from Uttarkashi). Another special place for the bird-watchers is the Har-ki-Doon Valley (54-km trek from Jarmola).

Flora and fauna

Uttarakhand has a diversity of flora and fauna. It has a recorded forest area of 34,666 km which constitutes 65% of the total area of the state. Uttarakhand is home to rare species of plants and animals, many of which are protected by sanctuaries and reserves.

Alpine Musk Deer (**Moschus chrysogaster**)

Himalayan Monal (**Lophophorus impejanus**)

National parks in Uttarakhand include the Jim Corbett National Park (the oldest national park of India) at Ramnagar in Nainital District, and Valley of Flowers National Park and Nanda Devi National Park in Chamoli District, which together are a UNESCO World Heritage Site.

West Himalayan Common Peacock(**Papilio bianor polyctor**)

Brahma Kamal (**Saussurea obvallata**)

Kaphal (**Myrica esculenta**)

A number of plant species in the valley are internationally threatened, including several that have not been recorded from elsewhere in Uttarakhand.Rajaji National Park in Haridwar District and Govind Pashu Vihar National Park and Sanctuary and Gangotri National Park in Uttarkashi District are some other protected areas in the state.

Burans **(Rhododendron arboreum)**

Leopards are found in areas which are abundant in hills but may also venture into the lowland jungles. Smaller felines include the jungle cat, fishing cat, and leopard cat. Other mammals include four kinds of deer (barking, sambar, hog and chital), sloth and Himalayan black bears, Indian gray mongooses, otters, yellow-throated martens, bharal, Indian pangolins, and langur and rhesus monkeys. In the summer, elephantscan be seen in herds of several hundred. Marsh crocodiles (*Crocodylus palustris*), gharials (*Gavialis gangeticus*) and other reptiles are also found in the region. Local crocodiles were saved from extinction by captive breeding programs and subsequently re-released into the Ramganga river. Several freshwater terrapins and turtles like the Indian sawback turtle (*Kachuga tecta*), brahminy river turtle (*Hardella thurgii*), and Ganges softshell turtle (*Trionyx gangeticus*) are found in the rivers. Butterflies and birds of the region include red Helen (*Papilio helenus*), the great eggfly (*Hypolimnos bolina*), common tiger (*Danaus *genutia*), pale wanderer (*Pareronia avatar avatar*), jungle babbler, tawny-bellied babbler, great slaty woodpecker, red-breasted parakeet, orange-breasted green pigeon and chestnut-winged cuckoo. In 2011, a rare migratory bird, the bean goose, was also seen in the Jim Corbett National Park.

Evergreen oaks, rhododendrons, and conifers predominate in the hills. *sal* (*Shorea robusta*), silk cotton tree (*Bombax ciliata*), *Dalbergia sissoo*, *Mallotus philippensis*, *Acacia catechu*, *Bauhinia racemosa*, and *Bauhinia variegata* (camel's foot tree) are some other trees of the region. *Albizia chinensis*, the sweet sticky flowers of which are favoured by sloth bears, are also part of the region's flora. A decade long study by Prof. Chandra Prakash Kala concluded that the Valley of Flowers is endowed with 520 species of higher plants (*angiosperms*, *gymnosperms* and *pteridophytes*), of these 498 are flowering plants. The park has many species of medicinal plants including *Dactylorhiza hatagirea*, *Picrorhiza kurroa*, *Aconitum violaceum*, *Polygonatum multiflorum*, *Fritillaria roylei*, and *Podophyllum hexandrum*. In the summer season of 2016, a large portion of forests in Uttarakhand caught fires and rubbled to ashes during Uttarakhand forest fires incident which resulted in the damage of forest resources worth billions of rupees and death of 6 people with hundreds of wild animals died during fires.

6

Economy

ECONOMY OF UTTARAKHAND

The Uttarakhand state is the second fastest growing state in India. It's gross state domestic product (GSDP) (at constant prices) more than doubled from 24,786 crore in FY2005 to 60,898 crore in FY2012. The real GSDP grew at 13.7% (CAGR) during the FY2005–FY2012 period. The contribution of the service sector to the GSDP of Uttarakhand was just over 50% during FY 2012. Per capita income in Uttarakhand is 1,03,000 (FY 2013) which is higher than the national average of 74,920 (FY2013). According to the Reserve Bank of India, the total foreign direct investment in the state from April 2000 to October 2009 amounted to US$46.7 million.

Like most of India, agriculture is one of the most significant sectors of the economy of Uttarakhand. Basmati rice, wheat, soybeans, groundnuts, coarse cereals, pulses, and oil seeds are the most widely grown crops. Fruits like apples, oranges, pears, peaches, litchis, and plums are widely grown and important to the large food processing industry. Agricultural export zones have been set up in the state for leechi, horticulture, herbs, medicinal plants, and basmati rice. During 2010, wheat production was 831 thousand tonnes and rice production was 610 thousand tonnes, while the main cash crop of the state, sugarcane, had a production of 5058 thousand tonnes. As 86% of the state consists of hills, the yield per hectare is not very high. 86% of all croplands are in the plains while the remaining is from the hills.

A woman winnowing rice, an important food crop in Uttarakhand.

Economy of Uttarakhand at a Glance

figures in crores of Indian rupees

Economy at a Glance (FY-2012)	In Indian rupees
GSDP (current)	95,201
Per capita income	1,03,000

Other key industries include tourism and hydropower, and there is prospective development in IT, ITES, biotechnology, pharmaceuticals and automobile industries. The service sector of Uttarakhand mainly includes tourism, information technology, higher education, and banking.

During 2005–2006, the state successfully developed three Integrated Industrial Estates (IIEs) at Haridwar, Pantnagar, and Sitarganj; Pharma City at Selaqui; Information Technology Park at Sahastradhara (Dehradun); and a growth centre at Sigaddi (Kotdwar). Also in 2006, 20 industrial sectors in public private partnership mode were developed in the state.

Uttarakhand Budget 2016-17: Main highlights

Uttarakhand Finance Minister Indira Hridayesh presented Uttarakhand Budget 2016-17 (UK Budget 2016-17)

1. Receipts: Total revenue receipts of 2016-17 is estimated to be Rs. 32275.87 crore.

Total receipts in financial year 2016-17 estimated to be Rs. 39912.00 crore.

2. Expenditure: Total expenditure in financial year 2016-17 estimated to be Rs.40422.20 crore.

Total expenditure in financial year 2016-17 estimated to be Rs. 32250.39 crore in revenue account and Rs. 8171.81 crore capital account.

Rs 11015.62 crore provision is made towards expenditures on salaries and allowances of the employees, considering the recommendation of the Seventh pay commission.

Plan expenditure is estimated to be Rs. 15931.60 crore approximately.

3. Deficit: Total fiscal deficit for year 2016-2017 Rs.510.20 crore.

AGRICULTURE

Mountain, and Himalayan agriculture specifically, deviates substantially from the kinds practiced in less precipitous altitudes. Hill farmers the world over have adapted to the difficult geography, and the terrain has likewise influenced cultural modes in mountain societies. Patterns of land ownership, subsistence vs. surplus production, and level of market penetration have also been decisively affected.

However, traditional Himalayan agricultural systems and knowledge base are being steadily eroded by market pressures, bringing both economic and cultural changes in Uttarakhand.

Age-old self-reliance has given way to dependency on imports from the productive plains, with their pesticide/chemical fertilizer-enhanced yields. Cultural domination from the plains also threatens Uttarakhand's traditional foods as an increasing taste for mill-polished rice is outcompeting mountain crops. Activists in the hills have responded with a Save the Seeds movement and are raising awareness about the need for agricultural biodiversity.

The following sites are recommended:

- Mountain Farming Systems - Comprehensive look at Farming in Uttarakhand
- Proceedings - International Symposium on Mountain Farming held November 2002 in Mussoorie
- ICIMOD - Mountain Agriculture Resources
- Jardhari & Kothari - Conserving Agricultural Biodiversity (Tehri)
- Agrobiodiversity - Article on the Future of Indian Agriculture (Kothari)
- UN Volunteers - Info on Beej Bachao Andolan
- Vandana Shiva - Research Foundation for Science, Technology & Ecology and the Navdanya Project
- Subsistence Strategies and Environmental Management - RS Negi in Cultural Dimension of Ecology
- Back to Traditional Farming - Humanscape (2001/1)

AGRICULTURAL DIVERSIFICATION

About agriculture, micro village-level studies have shown that about eighty per cent of the working population are engaged in crop agriculture and animal husbandry. Despite a very high cropping intensity, out of the total expenditure on food, the value of own produced food cereals, pulses, oilseeds etc., was thirty nine per cent only and the balance sixty one per cent of the food required was imported from other region.

This speaks of an agriculture characterized by poor productivity, low income and stagnation. What is needed is to reform the present mode of cropping in agriculture and animal husbandry sector. The neighbouring state of Himachal Pradesh, which has similar geographical conditions, has achieved high success through agricultural diversification. This has infect improved the socio-economic status of the households, and it has reduced the distress of the rural labour force from the hardship incurred due to out-migration.

Similarly, the diversification measures tend to increase stall-fed animal of improved crossbred cattle, which ultimately enhance income and employment opportunities. It reduces crop intensity through land tillage operations and lesser tillage causes lower soil erosion.

In agriculture, a twofold agricultural strategy is required. Where conditions are suitable for food-grain production, the stress must be to change from low-yielding coarse cereals and pulses to high-yielding rice and wheat. In other lands, the effort must be to shift from food-grains to high-value crops. The twin measures would go far towards solving the multiple problems of food, income and employment. This will of course require infrastructural support in the form of soil and water conservation measures, irrigation facilities, and credit and marketing support. In this regard, the zonal agro-climatic policy for Uttarakhand needs to be redrafted, focusing on the thrust areas for development. The adoption of these measures would reduce the rate of out-migration considerably.

GENERATION OF NON-FARM EMPLOYMENT

Agricultural diversification, if introduced, also provides opportunities for non-farm employment. The experience of

Himachal Pradesh could be a lesson for the Uttarakhand. Local employment in trade and business activities is invariably higher where diversification has taken place. To facilitate this developmental process, public policy should aim at providing basic infrastructure like roads, communication networks and market yards in the hills.

It has been observed that higher the degree of agricultural diversification, the lower is the direct employment of the family work force in agriculture. Vegetable and fruit cultivation creates greater manpower demand for grading, processing, packaging, transportation, marketing and management operations. The Himachal experience shows that vegetable cultivation has brought improvement in income, and a higher percentage of workers joined farm-related service sector.

LAND DEVELOPMENT ACTIVITIES

In the hilly parts, vast areas of barren land have wrongly been classified under forest cover, if the vast unused, barren and uncultivable lands are properly developed and utilized, it can become an important source of wealth for the hills. This task calls for considerable governmental help, involving the setting up of some agencies to identify and develop various types of land. Culturable waste would need to be made culturable.

Development of land in this manner would offer a better prospect of optimized land use with cropping pattern accommodating more perennial crops mixed with seasonal ones. If the spatial location technology and crop production technology are applied with the appropriate cropping at the right places, sustainable development will take place. Instead of migrating, potential migrants will then have access; locally available employment opportunities within the region through rural to rural migration.

TRANSPORT

Uttarakhand has 28,508 km of roads, of which 1,328 km are national highways and 1,543 km are state highways. The

State Road Transport Corporation (SRTC), which has been reorganised in Uttarakhand as the Uttarakhand Transport Corporation, is a major constituent of the transport system in the state. The Corporation began to work on 31 October 2003 and provides services on interstate and nationalised routes. As of 2012, approximately 1000 buses are being plied by the "Uttarakhand Transport Corporation" on 35 nationalised routes along with many other non-nationalised routes. There are also private transport operators operating approximately 3000 buses on non-nationalised routes along with a few interstate routes in Uttarakhand and the neighbouring state of U.P. For travelling locally, the state, like most of the country, has auto rickshaws and cycle rickshaws. In addition, remote towns and villages in the hills are connected to important road junctions and bus routes by a vast network of crowded share jeeps.

Jolly Grant Airport, Dehradun

The air transport network in the state is gradually improving. Jolly Grant Airport in Dehradun, is the busiest airport in the state with six daily flights to Delhi Airport. Pantnagar Airport, located in Pantnagar of the Kumaon region have 1 daily air service to delhi and return too . There government is planning to develop Naini Saini Airport in Pithoragarh, Bharkot Airport in Chinyalisaur in Uttarkashi district and Gauchar Airport in Gauchar, Chamoli district. There are plans to launch helipad service in Pantnagar and Jolly Grant Airports and other important tourist destinations like Ghangaria and Hemkund Sahib.

As over 86% of Uttarakhand's terrain consists of hills, railway services are very limited in the state and are largely confined to the plains. In 2011, the total length of railway tracks was about 345 km. Rail, being the cheapest mode of transport, is most popular. The most important railway station in Kumaun Division of Uttarakhand is at Kathgodam, 35 kilometres away from Nainital. Kathgodam is the last terminus of the broad gauge line of North East Railways that connects Nainital with Delhi, Dehradun, and Howrah. Other notable railway stations are at Pantnagar, Lalkuan and Haldwani.

Dehradun railway station is a railhead of the Northern Railways. Haridwar station is situated on the Delhi–Dehradun and Howrah–Dehradun railway lines. One of the main railheads of the Northern Railways, Haridwar Junction Railway Station is connected by broad gauge line. Roorkee comes under Northern Railway region of Indian Railways on the main Punjab – Mughal Sarai trunk route and is connected to major Indian cities. Other railheads are Rishikesh, Kotdwar and Ramnagar linked to Delhi by daily trains.

7

Tourism

TOURISM IN UTTARAKHAND

Uttarakhand is a state North Indian region of Himalayas. The state is popularly known as Devbhumi (land of Gods) due to the presence of numerous Hindu pilgrimage sites. As a result, religious tourism forms a major portion of the tourism in the state. The tourism business in Uttarakhand generated 23,000 crores during 2013-14.

View of a Bugyal (meadow) in Uttarakhand

Uttarakhand has many tourist spots due to its location in the Himalayas. There are many ancient temples, forest reserves, national parks, hill stations, and mountain peaks that draw large number of tourists. There are 44 nationally protected monuments in the state. Oak Grove School in the state is on the tentative list for World Heritage Sites. Two of the most holy rivers in Hinduism the Ganges and Yamuna, originate in Uttarakhand.

Gurdwara Hemkund Sahib, an important pilgrimage site for Sikhs

Uttarakhand has long been called "Land of the Gods" as the state has some of the holiest Hindu shrines, and for more than a thousand years, pilgrims have been visiting the region in the hopes of salvation and purification from sin.

Gangotri and Yamunotri, the sources of the Ganges and Yamuna, dedicated to Ganga and Yamuna respectively, fall in the upper reaches of the state and together with Badrinath (dedicated to Vishnu) and Kedarnath (dedicated to Shiva) form the Chota Char Dham, one of Hinduism's most spiritual and auspicious pilgrimage circuits.

Haridwar, meaning "Gateway to the God", is a prime Hindu destination. Haridwar hosts the Haridwar Kumbh Mela every twelve years, in which millions of pilgrims take part from all parts of India and the world. Rishikesh near Haridwar is known as the preeminent yoga centre of India. The state has an abundance of temples and shrines, many dedicated to local deities or manifestations of Shiva and Durga, references to many of which can be found in Hindu scriptures and legends. Uttarakhand is, however, a place of pilgrimage not only for Hindus.

Piran Kaliyar Sharif near Roorkee is a pilgrimage site to Muslims, Gurdwara Hemkund Sahib, Gurdwara Nanakmatta Sahib and Gurdwara Reetha Sahib are pilgrimage centers for Sikhs. Tibetan Buddhism has also made its presence with the reconstruction of Mindrolling Monastery and its Buddha Stupa, described as the world's highest at Clement Town, Dehradun.

Some of the most well-known hill stations in India are in Uttarakhand. Mussoorie, Nainital, Dhanaulti, Chakrata, Tehri, Lansdowne, Pauri, Sattal, Almora, Kausani, Bhimtal, and Ranikhet are some popular hill stations in Uttarakhand.

Auli and Munsiari are well-known skiing resorts in the state. The state has 12 National Parks and Wildlife Sanctuaries which cover 13.8 percent of the total area of the state.

They are located at different altitudes varying from 800 to 5400 metres. The oldest national park on the Indian sub-continent, Jim Corbett National Park, is a major tourist attraction. The park has varied wildlife and Project Tiger run by the Government of India.

Rajaji National Park is known for its elephants. In addition, the state boasts Valley of Flowers National Park and Nanda Devi National Park in Chamoli District, which together are a UNESCO World Heritage Site. Vasudhara Falls, near Badrinath is a waterfall with a height of 122 metres (400 ft) set in a backdrop of snow-clad mountains.

The state has always been a destination for mountaineering, hiking, and rock climbing in India. A recent development in adventure tourism in the region has been whitewater rafting in Rishikesh. Due to its proximity to the Himalaya ranges, the place is full of hills and mountains and is suitable for trekking, climbing, skiing, camping, rock climbing, and paragliding. Roopkund is a trekking site, known for the mysterious skeletons found in a lake, which was featured by National Geographic Channel in a documentary. The trek to Roopkund passes through the meadows of Bugyal.

CHAR DHAM

Uttarakhand is famous for Char Dham Yatra, which literally meaning 'journey to four centres'. These four religious centres in Uttarakhand are represented by Badrinath (dedicated to Lord Vishnu), Kedarnath(dedicated to Lord Shiva), Gangotri (the holy origin of river Ganga)and Yamunotri (the holy origin of river Yamuna).

The Char Dham Yatra begins around the first to second week of May every year. These dates are announced in the national media. The base for the yatra is generally the Rishikesh town which has all the amenities available for pilgrims and tourists alike. Pilgrims and tourists generally book their journey through the local travel agents to all the four locations.

BADRINATH

Badrinath is the abode of Lord Vishnu, who is called 'Badri Vishal', Badri the Big One. Legend has it that Badrinath was in fact the abode of Lord Shiva, who used to reside there with His consort Mother Parvati.

Lord Vishnu happened to like the place and wished to reside there permanently, so He took the form of an infant and started crying inconsolably. Mother Parvati's heart melted and she picked up the infant Vishu and started cradling Him.

The crying of the infant, however, disturbed the meditation of Lord Shiva and unable to bear the crying He left for higher reaches of the Himalayas and made Kedarnath His home. Once Lord Shiva left Mother Parvati too followed, which gave an opportunity to Lord Vishnu to take His original form and remain at Badrinath forever.

The priests of Badrinath are from the southernmost part of India, i.e. Kerala. This is according to the rules laid down by Adi Sankara. Badrinath remains out of bounds for pilgrims for 6 months a year, from October to May.

Badrinath Valley, along the Alaknanda River, Uttarakhand

Significance: Badrinath was established as a major pilgrimage site by Adi Shankara in the ninth century. Since then, its popularity has increased significantly, with an estimated 600,000 pilgrims visiting during the 2006 season, compared to 90,676 in 1961. The temple in Badrinath is also a sacred pilgrimage site for Vaishnavites.

Badrinath has been mentioned as a holy place in scriptures and legends for thousands of years. According to the Srimad Bhagavatam, "There in Badrikashram the Personality of Godhead (Vishnu), in his incarnation as the sages Nara and Narayana, had been undergoing great penance since time immemorial for the welfare of all living entities." (Srimad Bhagavatam 3.4.22)

Badri refers to a berry that was said to grow abundantly in the area, and nath refers to Vishnu. Badri is the Sanskrit name for the Indian Jujube tree, which has an edible berry. Some scriptural references also refer to Jujube trees being abundant in Badrinath. Legend has it that Goddess Lakshmi took the form of the berries to protect Lord Vishnu from the harsh climate during his long penance.

Badrinath Temple: The most visited site in the town of Badrinath is the Badrinath temple. The temple was built in the ninth century by Adi Shankara. Since then, it has undergone several major renovations, due to damage by avalanche. The temple now has a modern looking, colourful front, atypical of Hindu temples. Several murtis are worshipped in the temple. The most important is a one meter tall black stone image of Vishnu, as Lord Badri Narayan. The statue depicts Vishnu sitting in meditative posture, rather than His far more typical reclining pose.

History and Legend: One legend has it that when the goddess Ganga was requested to descend to earth to help suffering humanity, the earth was unable to withstand the force of her descent. Therefore the mighty Ganga was split into twelve holy channels, with Alaknanda one of them. It later became the abode of Lord Vishnu or Badrinath.

The mountains around Badrinath are mentioned in the Mahabharata, when the Pandavas are said to have ended their life by ascending the slopes of a peak in western Garhwal called Swargarohini - literally, the 'Ascent to Heaven'. Local legend has it that the Pandavas passed through Badrinath and the town of Mana, 4 km north of Badrinath, on their way to Swargarohini. There is also a cave in Mana where Vyas, according to legend, wrote the Mahabharata.

According to the Skanda Purana: "There are several sacred shrines in heaven, on earth, and in hell; but there is no shrine like Badrinath."

The area around Badrinath was celebrated in Padma Purana as abounding in spiritual treasures.

Badrinath has also been eulogised as Bhu Vaikunta or earthly abode of Lord Vishnu. Many religious scholars such as Ramanujacharya, Madhawacharya and Vedanta Desika visited Badrinath and wrote sacred texts, such as commentaries on Brahmasutras and other Upanishads.

Pilgrimage: Located only a few kilometres from the Indo-China (Tibet) border, Badrinath is generally a two-day-long journey from either Kedarnath, the site that precedes it in the Char Dham circuit, or one of the main disembarkation points on the plains. Hemkund Sahib, an important Sikh pilgrimage site, is on the way to Badrinath, so the road is especially crowded during the summer pilgrimage season. The temple and its substantial surrounding village are accessible by road.

There is a hot spring near the temple, and many saints live in the surrounding mountains all year round despite the harsh winter at such high elevations.

The northern math established by Adi Sankara is nearby at Jyotirmath. The best time to visit Badrinath is between June and September. Warm clothes are recommended all year.

Badrinath temple, sometimes called Badrinarayan temple, is situated along the Alaknanda river, in the hill town of Badrinath in Uttarakhand state in India. It is widely considered to be one of the holiest Hindu temples, and is dedicated to Lord Vishnu. The temple and town are one of the four Char Dham pilgrimage sites. It is also one of the 108 Divya Desams, holy shrines for Vaishnavites. The temple is open only six months every year (between the end of April and the beginning of November), due to extreme weather conditions in the Himalayan region.

Several murtis are worshipped in the temple. The most important is a one meter tall statue of Vishnu as Lord Badrinarayan, made of black shaligram stone. The statue is considered by many Hindus to be one of eight swayam vyakta keshtras, or self-manifested statues of Vishnu. The murti depicts Vishnu sitting in meditative posture, rather than His far more typical reclining pose. In November each year, when the town of Badrinath is closed, the image is moved to nearby Jyotirmath.

Temple History: Badrinath was originally established as a pilgrimage site by Adi Shankara in the ninth century. Shankara discovered the image of Badrinarayan in the Alaknanda River and enshrined it in a cave near the Tapt Kund hot springs. In the sixteenth century, the king of Garhwal moved the murti to the present temple.

The temple has undergone several major renovations, due to age and damage by avalanche. In the 17th century, the temple was expanded by the kings of Garhwal. After significant damage in the great 1803 Himalayan earthquake, it was rebuilt by the King of Jaipur.

Temple Description: The temple is approximately 50 ft. (15 metres) tall with a small cupola on top, covered with a gold gilt roof. The facade is built of stone, with arched windows. A broad stairway leads up to a tall arched gateway, which is the main entrance. The architecture resembles a Buddhist vihara (temple), with the brightly painted facade also more typical of Buddhist temples. Just inside is the mandapa, a large pillared hall that leads to the garbha grha, or main shrine area. The walls and pillars of the mandapa are covered with intricate carvings.

The main shrine area houses the black stone image of Lord Badrinarayan, sitting under a gold canopy. There are fifteen more murtis around the temple that are also worshipped. These include murtis of Nara & Narayana, Narasimha (the fourth incarnation of Vishnu), Lakshmi, Narada, Ganesha, Uddhava, Kubera, Garuda (the vehicle of Lord Narayan), and Navadurga.

Although Badrinath is located in the far north of India, the head priest, or Rawal, is traditionally from the far south of India, in Kerala. This tradition was begun by Adi Shankara. The Rawal is assisted by Dimripundits belonging to Village Dimmer of Garhwal.

The Tapt Kund hot sulphur springs just below the temple are considered to be medicinal—many pilgrims consider it a requirement to bathe in the springs before visiting the temple. The springs have a year-round temperature of 45°C.

History and Legend: Badrinath is mentioned in religious texts as far back as the Vedic period. Some accounts claim that the temple was built on a former Buddhist temple site.

One legend explains the reason that Vishnu is shown sitting in padmasana, rather than reclining. According to the story, Vishnu was chastised by a sage who saw Vishnu's consort Lakshmi massaging his feet. Vishnu went to Badrinath to perform austerity, meditating for a long time in padmasana.

To this day, the area around Badrinath attracts yogis who come for meditation and seclusion.

KEDARNATH

Kedarnath is the abode of Lord Shiva. Kedarnath is one of the 12 Jyotirlingams of India and the only one in the Uttarakhand. While there is a motorable road to Badrinath, Kedarnath could only be reached by foot. The 14 km trek begins from Gaurikund. After the 2013 Himalayan floods, the trek currently is of more than 18 km due to washing away of trekking paths.

Kedarnath

Kedarnath temple is one of the holiest Hindu temples dedicated to Lord Shiva located atop the Garwal Himalayan range near the holy river of Mandakini in Kedarnath, Uttarakhand in India. Due to extreme weather conditions, the temple is open only between the end of April to start of November. The temple is not directly accessible by road and has to be reached by a 13 km trek from Gaurikund down the hill. The temple is believed to have been built by Adi Sankaracharya and is one of the twelve Jyothirlingas, the holiest Hindu shrines of Lord Shiva. The temple is also one of the four major sites in India's pilgrimage - Char Dham.

Temple and Significance: The actual temple is an impressive stone edifice of unknown date. No specific family of pujaris supervises rituals at Kedarnath, which focus around veneration of the stone lingam that rests in the inner sanctum of the temple. Besides its affiliation with Shiva, Kedarnath is also believed to be the site of Shankaracharya's samadhi (achievement of beatified afterlife)

Surkanda Devi: Surkanda Devi is a Hindu temple situated close to the city of Dhanaulti and is at an altitude greater than 10000 ft. It is surrounded by dense forests and affords a scenic view of the surrounding cities (Dehradun, Rishikesh, etc.) The gange dussera festival is celebrated every year between May and June and attracts a lot of people.

It is located on a hill and one has to climb a steep 1.5 Km on foot after driving maybe to the foot of the hill.

Legend has it that the head of the charred body of Goddess Sati fell here when Lord Shiva was taking her remains along with him after she give her life in the yajna started by her father.

Accessibility: Kedarnath is accessible only after a steep 13 km trek through a paved path (horses or palanquins are available for rent) from Gaurikund, which is connected by road from Rishikesh, Haridwar, Dehradun and other important hill stations of the Garhwal and Kumaon regions in Uttarakhand. The temple is open only during the months of May to October, due to heavy snowfall and extreme cold weather during winter.

Demographics: As of 2001 India census GR India, Kedarnath had a population of 479. Males constitute 98% of the population and females 2%. Kedarnath has an average literacy rate of 63%, higher than the national average of 59.5%: male literacy is 63%, and female literacy is 36%. In Kedarnath, 0% of the population is under 6 years of age.

Mukteshwar: Mukteshwar is a town and tourist destination in the Nainital District of Uttarakhand, India, located at 29°302 003 N, 79°422 003 E. It sits high in the Kumaon Hills at an altitude of 2286 meters (7500 feet).

On the recommendation of the Cattle Plague Commission, the Institute then known as the Imperial Bacteriological Laboratory had its genesis on December 9, 1889 at Pune and later relocated to Mukteshwar in 1893 to facilitate segregation and quarantine of highly contagious organisms. Later it was developed into the Indian Veterinary Research Institute, which later moved its headquarters to Izzatnagar. Still Mukteshwar serves as the hill campus of IVRI, including various facilities such as an experimental goat farm.

Because of the hilly topography, agriculture in the area consists chiefly of potato fields and fruit orchards on terraces cut into the hillsides.

Mukteshwar is rich in scenic beauty, with magnificent views of the Indian Himalayas including India's highest peak, Nanda Devi.

Recently, the town is experiencing some construction activity and townships are mushrooming in and around Mukteshwar. Many people are buying holiday homes here to escape the chaos of large cities.

Munsiyari: Munsiyari is a Tehsil and a Sub Division of Pithoragarh district in the hill-state of Uttarakhand. India. Munsiyari, is at the base of the great Himalayan mountain range, and is a starting point of various treks into the interior of the Himalayas. It's name, when translated, refers to a 'place with snow'. Situated on the banks of Goriganga river, it is a fast growing tourist destination and Glacier enthusiasts, high altitude trekkers and nature lovers commonly use it as their hub or base camp. Munsiyari also falls on the ancient 'salt route' from Tibet and is at the entrance of the Johar valley which extends along the path of the Goriganga river to its source at Milam Glacier. It is inhabited mainly by the Shauka people (referred to as Bhotiya by the non-Shaukas), who are its original natives.

GANGOTRI

Gangotri is the origin of the holy river Ganga. River Ganga is revered as a mother throughout India. According to the Hindu philosophy, a place considered extremely holy if a river running through it flows in the northern direction. Gangotri is a place which is not only the origin of Ganga but also where Ganga flows in a northerly direction, hence the name 'Gangotri'. The river Ganga flows out from the melting Gangotri glacier, which is at a distance of around 18 km from the Gangotri town. Close to the temple is Bhagirath Shila, which according to the Hindu philosophy is the place where Bhagirath did penance for 5500 years to seek the blessings of Mother Ganga and requested her to descend to the Earth from her heavenly abode to cleanse the sins of his ancestors.

Pilgrimage: Gangotri, the source of the river Ganges and seat of the goddess Ganga, is one of the four sites in the Char Dham pilgrimage circuit.

Gangotri temple

The river is called Bhagirathi at the source and acquires the name Ganga from Devprayag onwards where it meets Alaknanda. The origin of the holy river is at Gaumukh, which is further 18 km trek along the Gangotri glacier. Gangotri can be reached in one day's travel from Rishikesh, Haridwar or Dehradun, or in two days from Yamunotri, the first site in the Char Dham circuit. More popular and important than its sister site to the east, Gangotri is also accessible directly by car and bus, meaning that it sees many more pilgrims than Yamunotri.

This small town is centred around a temple of the goddess Ganga, which was built by the Gurkha General Amar Singh Thapa in the early 18th century. The temple is closed on the Diwali day every year and is reopened in May. During this time, the idol of the goddess is kept at Mukhba village, near Harsil.

Ritual duties are supervised by the Semwal family of pujaris. The aarti ceremony at the Gangotri is especially impressive, as is the temple, a stately affair that sits on the banks of the rushing Ganga. Adventurous pilgrims can make an overnight 17 km trek to Gaumukh, the actual current source of the river Ganga.

For a large number of tourists, Gangotri town serves as the starting point of the Gangotri-Gaumukh-Tapovan and Gangotri-Kedartal trekking routes.

Mythological Relation: According to Hindu mythology, Goddess Ganga - the daughter of heaven, took the form of a river to absolve the sins of King Bhagirath's predecessors, following his severe penance of several centuries. Lord Shiva received Ganga into his matted locks to minimize the impact of her fall.

According to another legend, King Sagar, after slaying the demons on earth decided to stage in Ashwamegh Yagya as a proclamation of his supremacy. The horse which was to be taken on an uninterrupted journey around the earth was to be accompanied by the King's 60,000 sons born to Queen Sumati and one son Asmanjas born of the second queen Kesani. Indra, supreme ruler of the gods feared that he might be deprived of his celestial throne if the 'Yogya' (worship with fire) succeeded and then took away the horse and tied it to the ashram of Sage Kapil, who was then in deep meditation. The sons of the King Sagar searched for the horse and finally found it tied near the meditating sage. Sixty thousand angry sons of King Sagar stormed the ashram of sage Kapil.

When he opened his eyes, 60,000 sons had perished by the curse of sage Kapil. Bhagirath, grand son of King Sagar, is believed to have meditated to bring down the Ganga which brought back sixty thousand sons into life. The Bhagirathi 'Shila' is located near the temple of Ganga where the holy Ganga first descended on earth from heaven.

SUBMERGED SHIVLING

Bhavishya Badri Temple: Dense forests near Tapovan surround the Bhavishya Badri. The Bhavishya Badri is at a distance of about 17 km. east of Joshimath. Pilgrims trek beyond Tapovan up the Dhauliganga River to reach this holy spot. The idol of narsingha (the god with the head of lion) is enshrined here. Traditionally, it is believed that a day will come when the present route to the Badrinath will be inaccessible and the Lord Badrinath will be worshipped here and this is why the place is called Bhavishya Badri.

Demographics: As of 2001 India census[GRIndia], Gangotri had a population of 606. Males constitute 96% of the population and females 4%. Gangotri has an average literacy rate of 89%, higher than the national average of 59.5%: male literacy is 91%, and female literacy is 48%. In Gangotri, 0% of the population is under 6 years of age.

YAMUNOTRI

Yamunotri is the origin of the holy river Yamuna. A temple dedicated to the holy river Yamuna is situated at the place. The actual origin of the river is the Yamunotri glacier further up into the Himalayas where very few pilgrims go due to the difficulty it entails.

Yamunotri temple and ashram

PANCH KEDAR

Kedarnath

Tungnath

Rudranath

Madhyamaheshwar

Kalpeshwar

Panch Kedar

Panch Kedar refers to five Hindu temples or holy places of the Shaivite sect dedicated to god Shiva. They are located in the Garhwal Himalayan region in Uttarakhand, India. They are the subject of many legends that directly link their creation to Pandavas, the heroes of the Hindu epic Mahabharata.

The five temples designated in the strict pecking order to be followed for pilgrimage for worship are the Kedarnath at an altitude of 3,583 m (11,755 ft), the Tungnath (3,680 m or 12,070 ft), Rudranath (0A&M0(>%) (2,286 m or 7,500 ft), Madhyamaheshwar or Madmaheshwar (3,490 m or 11,450 ft) and Kalpeshwar (2,200 m or 7,200 ft). The Kedarnath is the main temple, which is part of the four famous Chota Char Dhams (literally 'the small four abodes/seats') or pilgrimage centers of the Garhwal Himalayas; the other three dhams are the Badrinath, Yamunotri and Gangotri. Kedarnath is also one of the twelve Jyotirlingas.

The Garhwal region is also called the Kedar-Khanda after Kedar — the local name for Lord Shiva. The region abounds in emblems and aniconic forms of Shiva sect of Lord Shiva, much more than the Vaishnava sect. The western part of this region in particular, which constitutes half of Chamoli district being known as Kedar-Kshetra or Kedar mandala, encompasses in its ambit all the five temples constituting the Panch Kedar.

Legend of Panch Kedar

The most famous folk legend about Panch Kedar relates to the Pandavas, the heroes of the Hindu epic Mahabharata. The Pandavas defeated and killed their cousins — the Kauravas in the epic Kurukshetra war. They wished to atone for the sins of committing fratricide (*gotra hatya*) and Brâhmanahatya (killing of Brahmins — the priest class) during the war. Thus, they handed over the reins of their kingdom to their kin and left in search of the god Shiva and to seek his blessings. First, they went to the holy city of Varanasi (Kashi), believed to Shiva's favourite city and famous for its Shiva temple. But,

Shiva wanted to avoid them as he was deeply incensed by the death and dishonesty at the Kurukshetra war and was, therefore, insensitive to Pandavas' prayers. Therefore, he assumed the form of a bull (Nandi) and hid in the Garhwal region.

Not finding Shiva in Varanasi, the Pandavas went to Garhwal Himalayas. Bhima, the second of the five Pandava brothers, then standing astride two mountains started to look for Shiva. He saw a bull grazing near Guptakashi ("hidden Kashi" — the name derived from the hiding act of Shiva). Bhima immediately recognized the bull to be Shiva.

Bhima caught hold of the bull by its tail and hind legs. But the bull-formed Shiva disappeared into the ground to later reappear in parts, with the hump raising in Kedarnath, the arms appearing in Tunganath, the nabhi (navel) and stomach surfacing in Madhyamaheshwar, the face showing up at Rudranath and the hair and the head appearing in Kalpeshwar.

The Pandavas pleased with this reappearance in five different forms, built temples at the five places for venerating and worshipping Shiva. The Pandavas were thus freed from their sins. It is also believed that the fore portions of Shiva appeared at Pashupatinath, Kathmandu — the capital of Nepal.

A variant of the tale credits Bhima of not only catching the bull, but also stopping it from disappearing. Consequently, the bull was torn asunder into five parts and appeared at five locations in the *Kedar Khand* of Garhwal region of the Himalayas. After building the Panch Kedar temples, the Pandavas mediated at Kedarnath for salvation, performed yagna (fire sacrifice) and then through the heavenly path called the Mahapanth (also called Swargarohini), attained heaven or salvation.

After completing the pilgrimage of Lord Shiva's darshan at the Panch Kedar temples, it is an unwritten religious rite to visit Lord Vishnu at the Badrinath Temple, as a final affirmatory proof by the devotee that he has sought blessings of Lord Shiva.

Devprayag

Rudraprayag

Karnaprayag

Nandaprayag

Vishnuprayag

Panch Prayag

Panch Prayag is an expression in Hindu religious ethos, specifically used to connote the five sacred river confluences in the Garhwal Himalayas in the state of Uttarakhand, India. The five *prayags* - prayag meaning "confluence" in Sanskrit - also termed as "Prayag pentad", namely the five river confluences, are Vishnu Prayag, Nand Prayag, Karn prayag, Rudra Prayag and Dev Prayag, in the descending flow sequence of their occurrence.

Vishnu Prayag

The Alaknanda River, which originates in the eastern slopes of glacier fields of Chaukhamba, is joined by the Saraswathi River near Mana (that originates on the south from the international border), and then flows in front of the Badrinath temple, one of the most revered Hindu shrines. It then meets the Dhauli Ganges River, whose origin is from the Niti Pass, after traveling a distance of 25 km (15.5 mi) from its source to form the Vishnu Prayag (30°332453N 79°342313E). This stretch of the Alaknanda River is called the Vishnu Ganges. Legend narrates the worship offered by sage Narada to god Vishnu at this confluence. An octagonal shaped temple - located near the confluence - dated to 1889, is credited to Maharani of Indore - Ahalyabai. Though originally built to install a Shiva linga, it now houses a Vishnu image. A stairway from this temple leads to the Vishnu kund (kund means pool of water or lake) at the confluence, which is seen in a tranquil state.

Nanda Prayag

Nand Prayag (30°192563N 79°182553E) is the second prayag in the cascade sequence of the confluences where the Nandakini River joins the main Alaknanda River. According to one tale, a noble King Nanda performed Yagnya (fire-sacrifice) and sought blessings of God. Hence, the confluence is named after him. The other version of the legend states that the confluence derives its name from the Yadava king Nanda, the foster-father of god Krishna. According to the legend, Vishnu granted a boon of the birth of a son to Nanda and his wife Yashoda and also the same boon to Devaki, wife of Vasudeva. Placed in a dilemma, since both were his disciples, he ensured that Krishna, an incarnation of Vishnu, was born to Devaki and Vasudeva but was fostered by Yashoda and Nanda. There is temple for Gopal, a form of Krishna, here. The legends also narrate that sage Kanva did penance here and also that wedding of King Dushyanta and Shakuntala took place at this venue.

Karna Prayag

Karn Prayag (30°152493N 79°122563E) is the location where Alaknanda River is joined by the Pindar River that originates from the Pindar glacier, below the Nanda Devi hill range.The epic Mahabharata legend narrates that Karna did penance here and earned the protective gear of *Kavacha* (armour) and *Kundala* (ear rings) from his father, the Sun god, which gave him indestructible powers. The name of the confluence is thus derived from the name of Karna. There is reference to this site in Meghaduta, a Sanskrit lyrical poetic drama written by the legendary poet Kalidasa, which attributes that Satopanth and Bhagirath glaciers joined here to form the Pindar River. Another classic work by the same author called the Abhijnana-shakuntala also mentions that Shakuntala and king Dushyanta's romantic daliance occurred here. It is also mentioned that Swami Vivekanandamediatated here for eighteen days.

The stone seat where Karna did penance is also seen here. A temple built in recent times to commemorate Karna has the deity of goddess Uma Devi (daughter of the Himalayas) here. The stone temple was rebuilt by guru Adi Shankaracharya. In the sanctum, the images of goddesss Parvati, her consort Shiva and her elepahant-headed son Ganesha are installed, next to that of Uma Devi, apart from Karna's image. A steep row of steps from the temple along a spur leads to the confluence point. And, down these steps, small shrines of Shiva and the *Binayak Shila* (the Ganesha stone) - that is believed to provide protection from danger - are located. Once in 12 years, a procession of the image of Uma Devi is taken round a few villages in the sub-divisional town of Karnaprayag.

Rudra Prayag

At Rudra Prayag (30°172163N 78°582433E) the Alaknanda meets the Mandakini River. The confluence is named after god Shiva, who is also known as Rudra. According to a widely narrated legend, Shiva performed the Tandava here, Tandava is a vigorous dance that is the source of the cycle of creation, preservation and dissolution. Shiva also played his favourite musical instrument the Rudra veena here. By playing the Veena, he enticed god Vishnu to his presence and converted him to water.

Another legend narrates that sage Narada had become conceited by his Veena playing skills. The gods requested Krishna in order to set things right. Krishna told Narada that Shiva and his consort Parvati were impressed by his musical talent. Narada was taken in by the praise and immediately set out to meet Shiva in the Himalayas. On the way at Rudra Prayag, he met several beautiful damsels called raginis (musical notes) who were disfigured and the reason for such disfigurement was squarely attributed to Narada playing his Veena. Hearing this, Narada felt humbled and surrendered before Shiva and decided to devote himself to learning music as disciple of Shiva.

According to another legend, the consort of Shiva - Sati was reborn as Parvati as the daughter of Himalaya, after she self-immolated herself in protest of the insult of Shiva. In spite of Himalaya's protests, Parvati performed rigorous penance to get the boon of becoming Shiva's wife in the new birth too.

Temples dedicated to Rudranath (Shiva) and goddess Chamunda are located here.

Dev Prayag

Dev Prayag (30°082433N 78°352523E) is the confluence of the two holy rivers, the Bhagirathi - the chief stream of the Ganges and the Alaknanda. It is the first prayag on the way to Badrinath. Beyond this confluence, the river is known as Ganges. The holiness of this place is considered equal to the famous Triveni sangam confluence at Allahabad where the Ganges, Yamuna and Saraswati rivers merge.

The confluence of the Bhagirathi, which flows in rapids with strong currents meets a much calmer river in the Alaknanda and this has been vividly described by the British captain Raper as:

The contrast between the two rivers joining here is striking. The Bhaghirathi runs down a steep declivity with rapid force, roaring and foaming flowing over large fragments placed in its bed, while the placid, Alakananda, flowing, with a smooth, unruffled surface, gently winds round the point till, meeting with her turbulent consort, she is forcibly hurried down, and unites her clamours with the blustering current.

Other Attractions

Rishikesh

Rishikesh has been a magnet for spiritual seekers since late 60's when The Beatles rocked up Maharishi Mahesh Yogi's ashram. Known as the 'Yoga Capital of the World' because of the large number of ashrams teaching meditation and yoga. The northern part of the main town is the hotspot for all the action where the Ganges forested hills form a conducive environment for all the meditation. The evening aarti also draws a lot of crowd.

Haridwar

Haridwar is an important city in the religious architecture of the country. The large number of people gathering on the bathing ghats on the holy ganges river give the place a chaotic feel. There are a number of Hindu temples, ashrams and dharamshalas (pilgrims' rest houses) in the city. The city also serves as the entry point to the nearby Rajaji National Park.

Fairs and festivals

Haridwar Kumbh Mela (fair) is a major tourist attraction to the state. Haridwar is one of the four places in India where this takes place. Haridwar also has its big annual fair in the form of Magh mela in January–February which turns into a bigger event every 6 years in the form of Ardh Magh Mela. Nanda Devi Mela and Nanda Devi Raj Yatra are great festivals of Uttarakhand, famous in all northern India. Nanda Devi Mela and Raj Yatra are the festivals of the goddess Nanda Devi, the bless-giving goddess. Kumaoni Holi a region variant of the Hindu festival of Holi is also very well known.

Wildlife

Uttarakhand is home to the Jim Corbett National Park, the first national park in India. There are 12 National Parks and Wildlife Sanctuaries covering 13.8 percent of the total area of the state. Nanda Devi Biosphere reserve and Valley of Flowers National Park are UNESCO World Heritage sites.

MOUNTAINEERING AND TREKKING

Trekking in the Darma valley region was formerly restricted by India's. Trekking without "inner-line" permits is currently (as of 2002) allowed to Panch Chuli base or Meola glacier. Additional permits may be required for other areas. For Trekking: Permits for Indian citizens can be obtained from SDM Dharchula or DM Pithoragarh. They need to carry their identity proof. For foriegners, the Ministry of Home Affairs, New Delhi will issue Inner line permits up to Bidang to cross into Kuti valley over Sin la. Beyond Bidang and towards Dawe it's strictly off limits for foreigners as the area has a 'sensitive' border with Tibet.

Gangotri Glacier

Gangotri Glacier is located in Uttarakhand, India in a region bordering China. The glacier is about 30 km long (19 miles) and 2 to 4 km (1 to 2 miles) wide. The terminus of the Gangotri Glacier is said to resemble a cow's mouth, and the place is called Goumukh (gou, cow + mukh, face). Goumukh, which is about 18 km (11 miles) from the town of Gangotri, is the precise source of the Bhagirathi river, an important tributary of the Ganga. Goumukh is situated near the base of a mountain called Shivling.

The Gangotri glacier is a traditional Hindu pilgrimage site. Devout Hindus consider bathing in the icy waters near Gangotri town to be a holy ritual, and many make the trek to Goumukh. The Gangotri glacier is roughly 30 km (19 miles) long. In recent times, it has been pointed out that the retreat of the glacier has quickened significantly.

Kali River: The Kali River originates from the Greater Himalayas at Kalapaani at an altitude of 3600 m, in the Pithoragarh District of Uttarakhand, India. The river is named after the Goddess Kali whose temple is situated in Kalapaani near the Lipu-Lekh pass at the border between India and Tibet. On its upper course, this river forms India's continuous eastern boundary with Nepal.

The Kali river joins with the Gori Ganga at Jauljibi, a place famous for its annual trade fair. It the joins with the Saryu river at Pancheshwar. The area around Pancheshwar is called 'Kali Kumaon'. Kali descends in plains and called by the name of Sharda.

The Pancheswar Dam, a joint venture with Nepal for irrigation and hydro-electric power generation will soon be constructed on the Kali. The Tanakpur Hydroelectric Project is also being built by the Uttarakhand Irrigation Department, with a dam on the river near the town of Tanakpur in the district of Champawat.

The Kali river is the part of the Ganges River System.

Kamet

Kamet is the second highest mountain in the Garhwal region of India, after Nanda Devi, 7,816 m (25,643 ft). It lies in the Chamoli District of Uttarakhand, close to the border with Tibet. It is the third highest mountain in India, and the 29th highest in the world. Kamet is most properly considered part of (and the highest summit in) the Zaskar (or Zanskar) Range, which lies north of the main chain of the Himalaya, between the Suru River and the upper Karnali River. In appearance it resembles a giant pyramid topped by a flat summit area with two peaks.

Climbing: Due to its position near the Tibetan Plateau, Kamet is remote and not as accessible as some Himalayan peaks. It also receives a great deal of wind from the Plateau. However, by modern standards, it is a relatively straighforward ascent for such a high mountain. Early explorers of the region faced long approach marches of around 200 miles from Ranikhet through dense mountain forest; access is easier today.

While attempts to climb Kamet began in 1855, the first ascent was not made until 1931 by Frank Smythe, Eric Shipton, R.L. Holdsworth and Lewa Sherpa, members of a British-Nepalese expedition. Kamet was the first summit over 25,000 ft (7,620m) to be climbed, and was the highest summit reached until the first ascent of Nanda Devi five years later. (However, far higher non-summit altitudes had been reached on the north side of Mount Everest in the 1920s.)

The standard route begins from the East Kamet (or Purbi Kamet) Glacier, ascending via Meade's Col (c. 7,100m/23,300 ft), the saddle between Kamet and its northern outlier Abi Gamin.

From Meade's Col the route ascends the northeast edge of the north face. The ascent to Meade's col involves steep gullies, a rock wall, and several glacier climbs. Five camps are usually placed en route. The final ascent to the summit involves steep snow, possibly icy.

Neighboring Peaks: Kamet is surrounded by three principal neighbours:

- Mukut Parbat, (two summits) 7,242 m (23,760 ft)/7,130 m (23,392 ft), 30°572 083 N, 79°342 133 E, northwest of Kamet. First ascent 1951 (see below).
- Abi Gamin, 7,355m (24,130 ft), 30°552 573 N, 79°362 093 E, north-northeast of Kamet; connected to Kamet by Meade's Col. First ascent 1950.
- Mana, 7,272m (23,858 ft), 30°522 523 N, 79°362 573 E, south-southeast of Kamet. First ascent 1937.

Several adjoining peaks, such as Mana NW, 7,092 m, Point 6,977 m, Deoban, 6,855 m, and Bidhan, 6,520 m, also lie close to Kamet.

Nomenclature: There are varying explanations of the name "Kamet." C. F. Meade gives the pronunciation as "Kumat" (u as in cut and a as in pay), and claims that it is known to Tibetans as Kangmen, signifying "huge grandmother of a sacred snow chain". However, Frank Smythe writes in his book Kamet Conquered that the genesis of the name is from the Tibetan word Kangmed ("the lower snows", from kang, "snow", and med, "little"), as distinct from the "higher snows" of the Kailash range, 110 miles east of Kamet. (This range is slightly lower than Kamet, its highest peak being Gurla Mandhata, 7,728 m/25,355 ft; however it stands more fully on the high Tibetan Plateau). At dawn and dusk, "the copper coloured rock of Mount Kamet reflecting the oblique rays of the sun on its hanging glaciers appears to set these glaciers aglow with crackling flames and bathes the mountain in a red burning glow". Hence the term "glacier fire" is also used as an allusion to the name Kamet.

Partial Timeline

- 1848: Richard Strachey determines the height and location of Kamet, as well as the neighbouring peaks Abi Gamin, Mukut Parbat, and Mana.
- 1855: German explorers and scientists Adolphe and Robert Schlagintweit, invited by the East India Company to make surveys, travel into Tibet in disguise. After being discovered and arrested, they return, and attempt Abi Gamin from Tibet (via the Abi Gamin Glacier), believing it to be Kamet. (This mistake hampers expeditions until 1912.) They claim to reach a height of 6,785 m (22,260 ft), which is extraordinary for this date.
- 1877: I. S. Pocock of the Survey of India, under E. C. Ryall, accurately surveys Kamet's position. However he supports the inaccurate belief that Abi Gamin is a minor subpeak of Kamet and that a northern route to the summit is practical.
- 1907: Dr. T. G. Longstaff, Brig. Gen. C. G. Bruce and A. L. Mumm, with alpine guides Alexis and Henri Brocherel, make a preliminary reconnaissance of the eastern and western sides of Kamet. The highest point reached is 6,100 m (20,000 ft) above the East Kamet Glacier. Longstaff deems the East Kamet route as too dangerous due to avalanche risk.
- 1910-1911: C. F. Meade, with Alpine guides Alexis Brocherel and Pierre Blanc, and a separate expedition under Dr. A. M. Kellas, make a preliminary reconnaissance of the western side of the peak; they explore Khaiam Pass and Glacier.
- 1911: Capt. A. M. Slingsby attempt Kamet on the western side from Ghastoli Glacier (or West Kamet Glacier) via the col on the ridge between Abi Gamin and Mukut Parbat (subsequently named as Slingsby's Col, 6,400 m/ 21,000 ft).
- 1912: Meade, with Alpine guides Pierre Blanc, Franz Lochmatter, Justin Blanc and Jean Perrin, attempts

Kamet by Slingsby's route, and also later explores the Raikhana glacier system to the east of Kamet. Meade concludes that the East Kamet Glacier is the only practicable route to Mt Kamet's summit.

- 1913: Slingsby attempts the same route as in 1911 and reaches 7,000 m (23,000 ft). (He later dies in battle in Mesopotamia in 1916.)
- 1913: Meade, with Alpine guide Pierre Blanc, attempts Kamet from the eastern side and reaches Meade's Col, 7,150 m (23,500 ft).
- 1914: Kellas makes another reconnaissance of which no records are available, and which is probably abandoned midway due to the commencement of World War I.
- 1920: Kellas and Col. H. T. Morshead attempt Meade's 1913 route and reach a point slightly above Meade's Col.
- 1931: The first ascent of Kamet, detailed above.
- 1937: Frank Smythe returns to the Bhyundar Valley and makes the first ascent of Mana, from its south ridge through the plateau at the head of the Uttari Naktoni glacier.
- 1950: An Anglo-Swiss expedition ascends Abi Gamin from its North East ridge.
- 1951: Mukut Parbat is climbed via the steep northwest ridge by a crack New Zealand team that includes Edmund Hillary, George Lowe, H. E. Riddiford as leader, F. M. Cotter and Pasang Dawa Lama.
- 1995: Mana Northwest is scaled by members of a joint Indo Tibetan Border Police–Japanese expedition after a tough technical wall climb.
- 2006: A commemorative 75th anniversary expedition by the Kolkata Section of the Himalayan Club puts ten climbers on the summit of Kamet. (First ascensionist Frank Smythe was a Himalayan Club member.)

Glaciers and Rivers: The West (Pachmi or Paschimi) Kamet Glacier, the East (Purbi or Purva) Kamet Glacier and the

Raikana Glacier systems surround Kamet. The branches of the West Kamet Glacier head on the western slopes of Kamet, Abi Gamin, and Mukut Parbat. The East Kamet Glacier flows from the eastern side of Kamet and Mana. The Raikhana glacier originates on the east side of Meade's Col saddle, flows east of Abi Gamin, and unites with the East Kamet Glacier. The West Kamet Glacier drains into the Saraswati River while the East Kamet Glacier feeds the Dhauli Ganga River; both rivers are tributaries of the Alakananda River, the major river of the Chamoli district.

High Altitude Research: A. M. Kellas and his companion H. T. Morshead conducted scientific studies during their 1920 Kamet expedition focusing on the physiology of high altitude travel and acclimatization, and on the possibility of using artificial oxygen. These studies eventually proved useful on expeditions to Mount Everest.

Pindari Glacier

The Pindari Glacier is a glacier found in the upper reaches of the Kumaon Himalayas, to the southeast of Nanda Devi. The trail to reach the glacier crosses the villages of Saung, Loharkhet, over the Dhakuri pass, onto Khati village (the last inhabited village on the trail), Dwali, Phurkia and finally Zero Point, Pindari, the end of the trail. Most of the trail is along the banks of the Pindari river.

The Pindari Glacier trail provides for a 90 Km (56 mile) round-trip trek that most people find comfortable to complete in five days. With the town of Bageshwar as base, take a bus or car to Saung, where the walk begins. One can camp overnight along the way or use the P.W.D. rest houses.

Ramganga

Ramganga West river originates from Doodhatoli ranges in the district of Pauri Garhwal, Uttarakhand state of India. The river Ramganga drains southwestern Kumaon Himalaya. It is a tributary of the river Ganga, originates from the high altitude zone of 800m-900m. Ramganga flows by the Corbett National Park near Ramnagar of Nainital district from where it decends upon the plains. Bareilly city of Uttar Pradesh is situated on it's banks. There is a dam across this river at Kalagarh for irrigation and hydroelectric generation. An annual festival of Ganga Dassahra is organised on it's banks annually during the months of September and October at Chaubari village near Bareilly.

Ramganga East: An another Ramganga called Ramganga East originates from the Namik glacier in Pithoragarh district of Uttarakhand and flows towards East. The river is fed by numerous small and big rivers and finally joins river Sarju at Rameshwar near Ghat of Pithoragarh. This river finally confluences with River Kali.

Siwalik Hills

The Siwalik Hills (also spelled Shiwalik, Shivalik, or Sivalik) are the southernmost and geologically youngest foothills running parallel to the main Himalayas. The Siwalik is a relatively low-altitude mountain range cresting at 900 to 1,200 meters. They extend 1,600 km from the Teesta River in Sikkim, westward through Nepal and Uttarakhand, continuing into Jammu and Kashmir. The Mohan Pass is the principal pass accessing the Siwalik Hills from Saharanpur in Uttar Pradesh to Dehra and the hill station of Mussoorie in Uttarakhand.

The Siwalik Hills are chiefly composed of sandstone and conglomerate formations which are the solidified and upheaved detritus of the great range in their rear, but often poorly consolidated. Sivapithecus (a kind of ape, formerly known as Ramapithecus) is among many fossil finds in the region.

Immediately south of these low mountains is an alluvial belt called the Terai, which apparently means "marshland" in Persian. This zone has many springs fed by monsoon rains falling on the uplands and absorbed into interspaces of the sedimentary rocks. This moist area was heavily malarial before DDT was used to suppress mosquitos, North of the Siwalik belt lies another range of foothills, the somewhat higher (1,500-3,000 meter) Mahabharata Lekh (Range) (in Nepal) also known as the Lesser Himalaya or the Middle Himalaya, although in many places valleys 10-20 km wide separate the Siwalik and Middle Himalaya ranges.

These valleys are called Duns or Doons in India (for example the Doon Valley) which includes Dehradun, as also Patli Dun and Kothri Dun, both in Corbett National Park in Uttarakhand, and also Pinjore Dun in Himachal Pradesh. In Nepal, they are part of the Inner Terai (for example Chitwan, Dang, Deukhuri and Surkhet).

The permeable sediments and poorly-developed soils of the Siwalik hills do not retain water between storms and are unsuited to agriculture. They are lightly populated by a few tribal groups, especially the Van Gujjars, or Gujjars, that follow a quasi-pastoral livestock-dependent lifestlyle and are responsible for heavy deforestation and denudation in many parts, given that the size of their herds has dramatically outgrown the ecosystems' capacity to sustain them.

Yamuna: Yamuna sometimes called Jamuna or Jumna) is a major river of northern India, with a total length of around 1370 km. It is the largest tributary of the Ganga. Its source is at Yamunotri, in the Uttarakhand Himalaya, which is north of Haridwar in the Himalayan Mountains. It flows through the states of Delhi, Haryana and Uttar Pradesh, before merging with the Ganges at Allahabad. The cities of Delhi, Mathura and Agra lie on its banks. The major tributaries of this river are the Tons, Chambal, Betwa, and Ken; with the Tons being the largest. A canal is currently being built between the Sutlej and Yamuna rivers, known as the SLY (Sutlej-Yamuna Link).

Wildlife and Surroundings: A little known fact about the Yamuna is that it is the frontier of the Asian Elephant. West of the Yamuna, there are no elephants to be found over 900 km of the western Himalayas and their foothills. The forests of the lower Yamuna offer ideal corridors for elephant movement. The principal forests to be found here are of Sal, Khair (Acacia), and

Sissoo (Rosewood) trees, and the Chir Pine forests of the Shivalik Hills.

Pollution: Yamuna is one of the most polluted rivers in the world. Especially in New Delhi, the capital of India and the areas near it. Though numerous attempts have been made to clean it, the efforts have proven to be futile. The main reasons for this is due to high density of population living in Delhi, the dumping of untreated water and solid waste into it (mostly illegally), the lax attitude of the government and mismanagement of projects focused at cleaning it. Also the water in this river remains stagnant for almost 9 months in a year aggravating the situation. Delhi alone contributes around 3,296 MLD (million litres per day) of sewage in the river.

The Govt. of India over the next five years has prepared plans to rebuild and repair the seweage system and the drains that empty into the river. To address river pollution, certain measures of cleaning river have been taken by the Ministry of Environment and Forests (MoEF) of the Government of India (GOI) in 12 towns of Haryana, 8 towns of Uttar Pradesh, and Delhi under an action plan (Yamuna Action Plan-YAP) which is being implemented since 1993 by the National River Conservation Directorate (NRCD) of the Ministry of Environment and Forests.

The Japan Bank for International Cooperation (JBIC) is participating in the Yamuna Action Plan in 15 of the above 21 towns (excluding 6 towns of Haryana included later on the direction of the honourable Supreme Court of India) with soft loan assistance of 17.773 billion Japanese Yen (equivalent to about Rs. 700 crore INR) while GOI is providing the funds for the remaining 6 towns added later.

In 2005, award winning documentary Jijivisha was made on Yamuna.

8

Population and Religion

POPULATION OF UTTARAKHAND

Uttarakhand, in the past known as Uttaranchal is a state situated in north India. It is as often as possible insinuated as the Land of the Gods in view of various Hindu sanctuaries and journey pilgrimage centre everywhere throughout the state. The state is known for its terrific magnificence of the Himalayas, the Bhabhar and additionally the Terai. On 9 November 2000, this state was made from the Himalayan and associating northwestern regions of Uttar Pradesh.

It is separated into two divisions, Garhwal and Kumaon, with an entirety of 13 districts. The capital of the state is Dehradun, the biggest city out here. Archaeological evidences bolster the presence of individuals in the zone since old times.

Population Of Uttarakhand In 2018

As indicated by the 2011 enumeration of India, Uttarakhand had a population of 10,116,752 including 5,154,178 males and 4,962,574 females, with 69.45% of the population living in rural territories.

Talking about population, in order to check out the population of Uttarakhand in 2018, we need to have a look at the population of the past 5 years. They are as per the following:

1. 2013 – 10.14 Million
2. 2014 – 10.17 Million
3. 2015 – 10.22 Million
4. 2016 – 10.28 Million
5. 2017 – 10.32 Million

Predicting the 2018 population of Uttarakhand is not easy but we can get the idea after analysing the population from the year 2013 – 17. As we have seen that every year the population increases by approximate 0.036 Million people. Hence, the population of Uttarakhand in 2018 is forecast to be 10.32 Million + 0.036 Million = 10.356 Million. So, the population of Uttarakhand in the year 2018 as per estimated data is 10.356 Million.

Uttarakhand Population 2018 –10.356 Million. (estimated)

Demography Of Uttarakhand:

The local individuals of Uttarakhand are by and large called Uttarakhandi and once in a while particularly either Garhwali or Kumaoni relying upon their place of origin in either the Garhwal or Kumaon district. As indicated by the 2011 Census of India, the state has a population of 10,086,292, containing 5,137,773 males and 4,948,519 females, with 69.77% of the population residing in country ranges. It is the twentieth most crowded state of the nation, having 0.83% of the population on 1.63% of the land. The population density is 189 persons per square kilometer, having a 2001–2011 decade development rate of 18.81%. The crude birth rate in Uttarakhand is 18.6 with the aggregate fertility rate being 2.3. It has a child death rate of 43 and a death rate of 6.6.

Population Density And Growth Of Uttarakhand:

The population density is 189 persons per square kilometre. As indicated by the points of interest from Census 2011, the state has a population of 1.01 Crores, an extension from figure of 84.89 Lakh in the 2001 assessment. The total population growth in this decade was 18.81% while in before it was around

19.20%. The number of occupants in the state shapes 0.83 percent of India in 2011. In the year 2001, the figure was 0.83 percent. The growth rate of females was higher as compared to that of the males in 2001. In 2013, the state included an enormous number of individuals in its kitty with a figure of around 16 lakhs alone in a solitary year. The growth rate of population presently is around 18% and the population of the state is expanding at a quick pace.

Facts About Uttarakhand:

1. Like the majority of the country, cultivating is among the most important sections of the economy of Uttarakhand. Basmati rice, groundnuts and oil seeds are the most grown items. Common items like apples, peaches, litchis, and plums are by and large grown and fundamental to the food industry.
2. The official Languages are Hindi and Sanskrit. Garhwali, Kumaoni in like manner can be heard in Uttarakhand.
3. It is very much connected by roadways, rail and flying courses. Its huge air terminal is in Dehradun and it is known as Jolly Grant Airport.
4. The fundamental nourishment of Uttarakhand is vegetables with wheat, regardless of the way that non-veg sustenance is also served. A specific characteristic of the state cuisine is the usage of tomatoes and milk based things. Coarse grain with high fiber content is uncommonly regular in the state in light of the territory.
5. One of the noteworthy Hindu journeys, Haridwar Kumbh Mela occurs in Uttarakhand. Haridwar is one of the four spots in the country where this mela happens.

DEMOGRAPHICS

The native people of Uttarakhand are generally called Uttarakhandi and sometimes specifically either Garhwali or Kumaoni depending on their place of origin in either the Garhwal or Kumaon region. According to the 2011 Census of India, Uttarakhand has a population of 10,086,292 comprising

5,137,773 males and 4,948,519 females, with 69.77% of the population living in rural areas. The state is the 20th most populous state of the country having 0.83% of the population on 1.63% of the land. The population density of the state is 189 people per square kilometre having a 2001–2011 decadal growth rate of 18.81%. The gender ratio is 963 females per 1000 males. The crude birth rate in the state is 18.6 with the total fertility rate being 2.3. The state has an infant mortality rate of 43, a maternal mortality rate of 188 and a crude death rate of 6.6.

Ethnic groups

Uttarakhand has a multiethnic population spread across two geocultural regions: the Garhwal, and the Kumaon. A large portion of the population is Rajput (various clans of erstwhile landowning rulers and their descendants), including members of the native Garhwali, Kumaoni and Gurjar communities, as well as a number of immigrants. According to a 2007 study by Centre for the Study of Developing Societies, Uttarakhand has the highest percentage of Brahmins of any state in India, with approximately 20% of the population being Brahmin. 18.76% of the population belongs to the Scheduled Castes (an official term for the indigenous aboriginal lower castes in the traditional Hindu caste system).Scheduled Tribes such as the Tharu, Jaunsari, Buksa, Bhotiya and Raji constitute 2.89% of the population.

Languages

Languages in Uttarakhand (2011)

Hindi (89.15%)

Urdu (4.22%)

Punjabi (2.61%)

Bengali (1.5%)

Nepali (1.05%)

Other (1.47%)

Hindi belonging to Indo-Aryan languages is the sole official language of Uttarakhand and is spoken by 89.15% of the population (figure includes Garhwali spoken by 23.02%, Kumaoni spoken by 19.94% and Jaunsari spoken by 1.35% of the population as variants of Hindi). Sanskrit is given the status of second official language. Many Tibeto-Burman languages are also spoken in this region, including Jad, Rongpo, Darmiya, Byangsi, Chaudangsi, Raji and Rawat.

Religion

Religion in Uttarakhand (2011)

Hinduism (82.97%)

Islam (13.95%)

Sikhism (2.34%)

Christianity (0.37%)

Buddhism (0.15%)

Jainism (0.09%)

Other or not religious (0.13%)

More than four-fifths of Uttarakhand's residents are Hindus. Muslims, Sikhs, Christians, Buddhists, and Jains make up the remaining population with the Muslims being the largest minority.

UTTARAKHAND RELIGIONS

There's no doubt that religion is something that Indians can't live without. Though Hindus constitute the majority of Uttarakhand's population, the state also features many different faiths or systems of beliefs. The percentage of Hindus in the state is around 92%. The remaining population is comprised of people belonging to religions like Sikhism, Christianity and Islam among others. No wonder, all these people that follow different faiths live quite harmoniously with one another, which makes Uttarakhand one of the most beautiful and peaceful states in the country.

Apart from these major religions, you'll also notice some other forms of worships. Uttarakhand is also home to many different ethnic groups or sects that follow their own folk forms of worship. Some of these include Snake Worship, Karna Worship, Duryodhana Worship and Mahasu worship among others.

List of Uttarakhand Religions

Given below is a list of all the major religions that are followed and practiced in different cities and towns of the state of Uttarakhand. During your visit to the state, it's important to make sure that you respect the customs and traditions of every religion.

Hinduism

The predominant religion in the state of Uttarakhand is Hinduism. This religion consists the worship of Brahma, Shiva, Shakti, Vishnu, and other Gods and Goddesses.

Some of the famous Hindu religious places in Uttarakhand are - Rudranath Temple, Badrinath Temple, Gangotri Temple, Kedarnath Temple, Yamunotri Temple, Naina Devi Temple, etc.

More than 90% of population of Uttarakhand consists of Hindus. The other religions that can be found there are the following:

- Sikhs - 2.5%
- Muslims - 2.5%
- Christians - 2.5%

9

Art, Architecture, Fair and Festivals

ARTS & CRAFTS

The state of Uttarakhand has a rich tradition of various arts and crafts like painting, wood carving, jewelry making, candle making, decorative temples and of course performing arts like music and dance. Their inspiration was obviously the lush green surroundings, the turquoise sky and the snow filled mountains which could make anyone poetic. The tranquil environs form a base for a treasure-house of artistically inclined people.

The most prominent craft of Uttaranchal is wood carving. Every Garhwali home, let alone the palaces, has an intricately carved wooden entrance door. Talking of palaces, the most notable wood-carved architectural wonders are the Chandpur Fort, Temple of Srinagar (Garhwal), Pandukeshwar (near Badrinath), Devi Madin (near Joshimath), and Devalgarh Temple.

The next in line are the fine-arts including the Miniature Paintings and Aipan & Peeth.

The miniature paintings have Mughal influence but Uttaranchal has its own school/style of painting called the Garhwal School of Painting (offshoot of the Pahari School). Aipan and Peeth however are folk forms art made generally in homes and practiced usually by women. Both use a lot of geometric patterns, 'Geru' and rice paste. One can buy traditional Uttarakhand ornaments made from gold, silver, copper, beads, semi-precious stones and lacquer from various jewelry shops across the state.

Aipan

Rangoli, a traditional Indian art displayed in front of the house, makes up a sacred and age-old practice. Aipan is one of the conventional forms of rangoli, mainly practiced in the state of Uttarakhand. The art has cultural as well as religious implication in the life of the Kumanois.

Murals

The fine arts of Uttaranchal are decidedly geometric with a natural grace and simplified complexity. One will find almost every home and place of worship decorated with some kind of mural done either as a proper wall painting or in the form of Aipan and Peeth.

Paintings

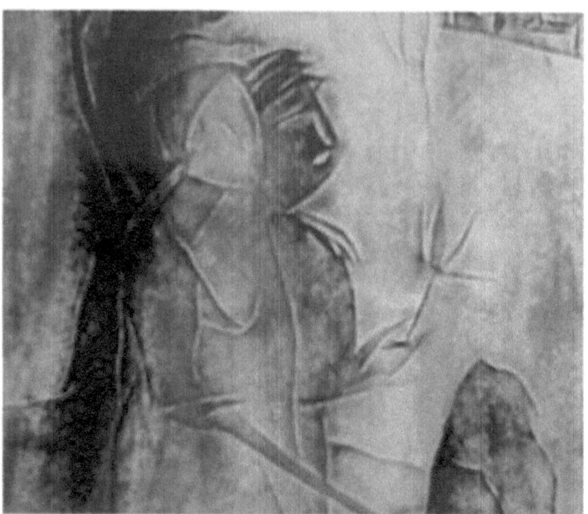

Uttarakhand is interspersed with lush green trees, towering mountains and a clear blue sky. These things are enough to make someone a poet or an artist.

This is just a fraction of the beauty of the hilly territory. Uttaranchal or specifically, Garhwal is home to one of the most beautiful and defining 'Gharanas' of miniature paintings known as the Garhwal School of Painting.

Temple Architecture

Temple architecture in any part of India has always been patronized by the kings and people ruling there as a way to leave an imprint on the pages of history. The rulers of yesteryears built some of the intricately carved and exquisite places of worship.

Wood Carving

The people of Uttaranchal are very creative in nature and the fact testifies itself in the beautiful temples that dot the entire land. The wood carvings of Garhwal and Kumaon are renowned for their simple yet delicate and attractive designs.

ARTS AND CRAFTS OF UTTARAKHAND

Uttarakhand, a mountainous state, enjoys special privilege for being that part of the subcontinent wherefrom the Indian Civilization actually developed and proliferated to the pan-Indian dimension. This region has therefore been the grand repository of diverse cultures since the intermingling of Khasa and Kirati cultures that took place here ages ago. The tradition of painting in Uttarakhand remained confined only to what earlier used to be the Garhwal kingdom. The art of Miniature Painting flourished in Garhwal under the influence of Mughal and Western Pahari schools, and that too without any feudal patronage. The arts and crafts of Uttarakhand, of which an amazingly rich variety exist, demand and indeed deserve a closer look.

Arts and Crafts of Uttarakhand - The Performing Arts

The performing arts of Uttarakhand like most other folk cultures in India, revolves around rustic music and dance. The colorful tribes and clans have their own indigenous dance forms which they perform with the accompaniment of local instruments and song. The Bhotiya Dance and the Langvir Dance are two commonly performed dances in Uttarakhand.

The Crafts of Uttarakhand

The arts and crafts of Uttarakhand are most popularly expressed in the crafts that have been practiced in Uttarakhand since ages now. The three areas in which the crafts of Uttarakhand are best reflected are:

Wood Carving :- The wood carving of the region is breathtaking for its simple beautiful designs. Wooden front doors carved with floral designs, animals & fishes standout for its simple beauty. The carving on one's front door is supposed to be symbolic of his prosperity. In Garhwal & Kumaon the facade of the upper storeys of the dwelling units are wooden and are artistically carved.

Paintings :- Garhwal, is famous for Mughal style of paintings. Apart from that, the folk Art known as aipana, is a speciality of Kumaon. It is a local adaptation of alpana, derived from the Sanskrit lip-to plaster with fingers is practiced by the women folk. The other schools or types of paintings practiced in this region are the pitha, the art form used to decorate the seat of Siva on auspicious days with geometrical patterns; and chowki the (seat) of Lakshmi and Saraswati using floral and traditional patterns.

Ornaments :- In every part of Garhwal and Kumaon, traditional goldsmiths make traditional ornaments using motifs and patterns thousands of years old. The ornaments come in variety of gold, silver, copper and brass.

KANDALI FESTIVAL

Kandali Festival is a festival held by the Bhotiya tribe of the Pithoragarh district of Uttarakhand state in India. This festival coincides with the blooming of the Kandali plant, which flowers once every twelve years. It is held in the Chaudas Valley between August and October. It celebrates the defeat of Zorawar Singh's army, which attacked this area from Laddakh in 1841.

The women go out in procession in their traditional attire to destroy the Kandali plants, where the soldiers were hidden. The demoralised army returned along the Kali River, looting the villages on the way. The women resisted them and this is re-enacted to this day. The festival includes dancing, feasting and partaking in the local brew 'Chakti'. Kandali last bloomed in 1999 and next festival will be held in 2011.

Kumbh Mela: Kumbh Mela is a Hindu pilgrimage that occurs four times every twelve years and rotates among four locations: Prayag (Allahabad), Haridwar, Ujjain and Nashik. Each twelve-year cycle includes one Maha Kumbh Mela (Great Kumbh Mela) at Prayag, which is attended by millions of people, making it the largest gathering anywhere in the world.

After visiting the Kumbh mela of 1895, Mark Twain wrote:

"It is wonderful, the power of a faith like that, that can make multitudes upon multitudes of the old and weak and the young and frail enter without hesitation or complaint upon such incredible journeys and endure the resultant miseries without repining. It is done in love, or it is done in fear; I do not know which it is. No matter what the impulse is, the act born of it is beyond imagination marvellous to our kind of people, the cold whites."

Astronomy and Kumbh Mela: The precise dates of the Kumbh Mela are astronomically determined, based upon precise calculations of the positions of the Sun, the Moon and Jupiter. At Prayag, the Maha Kumbh Mela is held in the month of Magha (January/February in the Gregorian calendar). The highest spiritual merit is attached to bathing on the new moon day, Amavasya, when Jupiter is in Taurus and both the Sun and Moon are in Capricorn. At Haridwar, the Kumbh Mela is held in the months of Phalgun and Chaitra (February/March/April), when the Sun passes to Aries, the Moon is in Sagittarius and Jupiter is in Aquarius.

In Ujjain, the festival is held in the month of Vaishakha (May), when other planets are in Libra, the Sun and Moon are in Aries and Jupiter is in Leo. At Nashik, the Kumbh Mela takes place in the month of Shravana (July), when the Sun and Moon are in Cancer and Jupiter is in Scorpio.

It is also said that the elixir of life is filled in a Kumbh (Pot) in Swarg (heaven) so with certain combination of Sun - Moon - Jupiter, the elixir falls from heaven to earth, and kumbh mela is held on those locations.

THE LEGEND

The observance of Kumbh Mela is based upon the following legend: Thousands of years ago, in the Vedic period, gods and demons made a temporary agreement to work together churning amrit (the nectar of immortality) from the Ksheera Sagara (primordial ocean of milk), and to share the nectar equally.

However, when the Kumbh (urn) containing the amrita

appeared, the demons ran away with it and were chased by the gods. For twelve days and twelve nights (equivalent to twelve human years) the gods and demons fought in the sky for possession of this pot of amrita. It is said that during the battle, drops of amrita fell at four places: Prayag, Haridwar, Ujjain and Nashik. Thus, the Kumbh Mela is observed at these four locations where the nectar fell.

RITUALS OF KUMBH MELA

Kumbh Mela is attended by millions of people on a single day. The major event of this festival is a ritual bath at the banks of the rivers in each town.

Other activities include religious discussions, devotional singing, mass feeding of holy men and women and the poor, and religious assemblies where doctrines are debated and standardized. Kumbh Mela (especially the Maha Kumbh Mela) is the most sacred of all the Hindu pilgrimages. Thousands of holy men and women (monks, saints and sadhus) attend, and the auspiciousness of the festival is in part attributable to this.

RECENT KUMBH MELAS

2003: When the Kumbh Mela was held in Nashik, India, from July 27 to September 7, 2003, 39 pilgrims (28 women and 11 men) were trampled to death and 57 were injured (keeping in mind that the number of devotees attending the fair was around 70 million). Devotees had gathered on the banks of the Godavari river for the maha snaan or holy bath. Over 30,000 pilgrims were being held back by barricades in a narrow street leading to the Ramkund, a holy spot, so the sadhus could take the first ceremonial bath. Reportedly, a sadhu threw some silver coins into the crowd and the subsequent scramble led to the stampede.

2007: Every twelve years there is an Ardh or half Mela at Prayag (also known as Allahabad) (2007). The actual dates are dependent on stellar constellations and were announced as below:

IMPORTANT BATHING DATES

- 3 Jan (Poush Purnima)
- 14 Jan (Makar Sankranti)
- 19 Jan (Mauni Amavasya)
- 23 Jan (Basant Panchami)
- 2 Feb (Magh Purnima)

IMPORTANT INFORMATION

Health Certificate : It is absolutely necessary that the pilgrims should get inoculated against Cholera and take a Certificate from any Government Health Centre. Other Certificates are not recognised by the Ardha Kumbha Mela Authority.

Warm Garments : Warm clothing should be taken. Mosquito net, torch light, water bottle are a must.

MASONARY AND ARCHITECTURE IN KUMAON

Kumaon has a distinctive style of architecture, which is to be seen on the one hand in scattered settlements of the higher Himalaya and populated agricultural valleys, and on the other in the temples, naulas-bawaris (water tanks), forts and dharamshalas (inns). Most of the old houses of Kumaon have stone walls, mud floors, slate roofs and patangans (courtyards of gray stone) and their doors, windows and Kholis (main entrance to the house) have intricate figures of Ganesh and other Gods - Goddesses.

The wood carver or carpenter never forgets to make closed nestles for birds. Although brick and concrete houses are now being constructed in Kumaon, very often, depending on the availability of the material, people still prefer to use stones, slate and wood for the construction of their houses.

The temples, which have been constructed over a period of about a thousand years, follow a local style known as the 'Himadri' style of architecture. The temples at Jageshwar, Almora, Katarmal, Thal, Baijnath, Someshwar, Dwarahat,

Gangolihat, Patal Bhuvaneshwar and Marsoli are very good examples of the local style, which is often termed as post Gupta architecture.

Along with architecture, Kumaon has also had a distinctive style of sculpture. One finds many idols in temples and even outside temples. The idols at Jageshwar, Dwarahat, Baijnath, Katarmal, Kasni and Champawat bear ample testimony to Kumaon's rich tradition of sculpture. The bronze or astdhatu statues are also worth seeing. Similarly, the Ek Hathia (literal meaning, 'one handed') Deval near Thal and the Ek Hathia Naula near Champawat are unusual expressions, not only because of the stories attached to their creation, but also from the point of view of their architectural design. A few statues bear influence of Buddhist art. The region is also rich in epigraphic and numismatic expressions.

There are Beerkhams or victory pillars (one piece) scattered all over Kumaon, and a few forts or ruins of various forts, are still to be seen at Almora, Champawat, Pithoragarh, Karnkarayat, Sira, Gangolihat and Kuti.

AIPAN AND OTHER ART FORMS

During the last two decades many rock paintings belonging to the protohistoric period have been discovered in Kumaon. Among them Lakhu Udiyar and Lwethaap are well known. The Pahari Kalam (style of painting) probably also developed in Kumaon, when it was being practiced in some of the Himalayan regions. Unfortunately very few examples of this style are available today.

The Aipan (Alpana) is a popular art form of Kumaon, and walls, papers and pieces of cloth are decorated by the drawing of various geometric and other figures belonging to gods, goddesses and objects of nature. Pichhauras or dupattas are also decorated in this manner. At the time of Harela there is a tradition of making clay idols (Dikaras).'Aepan' or Aipan or Alpana is an art which has a special place in all Kumaoni homes.

The word "Aepan' is a derivative of 'Arpan'. A commonly used word for it is "Likhai" (writing), although it is a pattern made with the fingers. Aepan are used as ritual designs for Pujas, festivals and ceremonies connected with birth, janeu (the sacred thread ceremony), marriage and death.

The raw material used is simple ochre colour and rice paste. It is mostly women who paint the designs on the floors and walls of their homes using the last three fingers of the right hand. Once the ochre base is ready the artist draws the pattern free hand. Chowkies are made with mango wood and painted with special designs for each occasion. Pattas & Thapas are made directly on the walls or on paper and cloth.

Earlier the paint used was made from natural 'dyes. Today, poster and oil paints both are used. We are using the traditional "patterns for cards, wall hangings, cushion covers, table cloths, even T-Shirts. The decorative patterns used to adorn doorways have been adapted for gift tags, bookmarks, clay items, wooden boxes, trays and coasters.

DIFFERENT FORMS OF AEPANS

1. *Saraswati Chowki:* Saraswati being the Goddess of learning, when a child begins formal education a puja is held to give him/her an auspicious start. The main feature of this chowki is a five-pointed star with a swastik flower or a diya in the centre. The artist then proceeds to decorate the centre piece with flowing designs or floral patterns
2. *Chamunda Hast Chowki:* This chowki is made for "havans" or "yagyas". Two triangles interspersed with two diagonal lines running across both, with a 5-pointed star in between, enclosed in a circle make the centre piece of this chowki. The gaps are filled up with floral designs or lakshmi's feet. The circle itself is often decorated with 8 petals of the lotus.
3. *Nav Durga Chowki :* Used for ritual Devi pujas. The main points here are nine dots representing the Nav Durgas. Those who are adept in aepan designs make a square

enclosing these dots with parallel lines running crisscross and decorate these with lotus petals. A simpler way is to form swastiks with the 9 dots, it is then called Nav Swastik. There are many variations of this. A simpler version is made by drawing three horizontal and vertical lines with a Swastik in the centre.

4. *Shiv or Shivarchan Peeth :* Shiv is the reigning God of the people of the Himalayas. He is worshipped specially in the months of Savan or Magh. 28 or 108 Parthiv Lings are placed in a copper thali and Shiv or Shivarchan Peeth is drawn on the ground. This is an eight cornered design with 12 dots joined by 12 lines. To make it more attractive there is an outside border of four plus four corners.
5. *The Surya Darshan Chowki :* It is connected with the naming ceremony of a newborn child. For eleven days the baby is kept indoors, on the eleventh day the child is brought outside for Surya Darshan. This chowki is made on the floor where the priest sits reciting mantras.
6. *Janeyu Chowki :* The chowki is made specially for the sacred thread ceremony. Seven stars within a six-sided drawing form the main section. The seven stars represent the Sapt Rishis. Around this floral designs with dots are drawn.
7. *Asan Chowki :* This is associated with the many kinds of chowkis used for various pujas. It is a decorated seat for the devotee and his wife for a ritual puja.
8. *Dhuli Arghya Chowki :* Twilight in India is called "Godhuli Vela" or the time when cows return home from the pastures. The dust which rises from their hooves gives the time its name. For weddings the bridegroom's party also arrives at the bride's house at this time of evening. In bygone days the bridegroom's entourage usually walked to the bride's place and so they arrived with dusty feet. Since the groom for this period represents "Narayan". God himself, so he is greeted with devotion. His dust covered feet are washed before the puja welcoming him

begins. He stands on a "Chowkil. or small stool on which is painted a tree like figure with three branches coming out on the top. It also resembles a pitcher with Shiva's Trishul or Trident on the top. At the base is Brahma the creator and in the middle Vishnu. On two sides of this painting, two parrots are painted and at the bottom the lotus as well as the Swastik. All three denote luck and are good omens.

9. *Acharya Chowki:* The groom is always accompanied among others by his own Pandit or Acharya. The Pandit is given more prominence than even the father of the groom. So a special chowki is made for him. A Swastik is made on it with red colour. The lotus and other auspicious symbols such as a bell, a conch shell, sometimes even 2 parrots are painted around the Swastik.

10. *Durga Thapa :* The Durga Thapa is painted on paper by the women of Kumaon for two Durga Pujas held during the year, one in March-April and the other before the festival of Dussehra. The pujas take place for nine days and are therefore caned Navratras.

    This Thapa or painting is highly complex. Almost an the gods and goddesses, besides several local deities are depicted along with the many-armed Durga who rides the lion. Ranking her on the left and right are the family deities of the Thakurs of Kumaon. Kot Kangra Devi and Jwala Devi. She is surrounded by auspicious symbols such as the conch shen, ben, lamp, tulsi, rice, grain and swastika. To her left are the Bhuja Bali gods. Ram and Lakshman. The twin sisters. Anayari and Ujyarl representing light and darkness and the goddesses worshipped at the hiji temples of Punyagiri and Dunagiri also find representation in this Thapa. On the right side are- the Nav Durgas and the nine headed Chandi Devi, with the temple guards at the bottom of the hierarchy. The topmost row in the painting features the sun, Ganesh - the elephant-headed god who is the remover of obstacles,

Riddhi, Lakshmi the goddess of wealth and her consort, Vishnu the Preserver in the Hindu Trinity; Brahma, the Creator and Saraswati the goddess of learning; local gods Gola Nath and Bhola Nath on horseback and Bala Barmi. The eight-petalled lotus within a circle is of special importance in a Durga Puja.

11. *Jyoti Patta :* In the hills of Kumaon, among the Brahmin and Sah families there is a practice of drawing a "Jyoonti" at a wedding or a sacred thread ceremony. In earlier times, "Jyoontis" were murals painted on the walls of rooms where religious ceremonies took place. These drawings are now made on paper, hardboard or plywood. Even printed Jyoonti Pattas are available. "Jyoonti" is the local word used for the Jeev Matrikas-Maha Laxmi, Maha Saraswati and Maha Kali. Worship of the Matrikas is an ancient tradition in Kumaon. The Bagnath Temple in Bageshwar has a panel of the Matrikas supposed to date back to the ninth century. The drawing of the "Jyoonti" or Jyoti Patta follows a pattern. The first line depicts the Himalayas because it is the practice to send the first invitation to them. Thereafter there are lines of floral or geometrical designs. One important panel has two lotuses on either side and a tree which symbolizes the mythical Kalpavriksha. Brahma, the Creator, and Vishnu, the Preserver, are said to reside in the roots of the tree, Shiva, the Destroyer, in its trunk and his consort, Parvati, in the topmost part of the tree. Below the tree, two parrots are painted for luck. In the centre of the panel are Radha-Krishna or Ganesh and Riddhi' or even the figures of the bride and groom.

    The main panel has the three Matrikas attended by Ganesh. On top, are the two circular faces of Anyari Devi and Ujyari Devi, the presiding deities over Light and Darkness. Ranking the central panel is an elaborate design of dots and lines called "Bar Boond". This represents an invocation as well as invitation to the gods to attend the wedding and bless the couple.

12. *Lakshmi Yantra :* In the hills of Kumaon as in other parts of India, the goddess of wealth, Lakshmi, is worshipped during the festival of Diwali. Before the idol is placed on the spot where the Puja will take place, the Lakshmi Yantra is drawn on the floor with ochre colour (Geru) and rice paste (Biswar). This is the seat of the goddess. The centre point of the Yantra is marked by a dot or flower, which symbolizes the Universe. It is enclosed in two triangles, which form a star with six points. The upper triangle represents Shiva and the lower one, Shakti. The triangle is encircled with six or eight lotuses. There can also be an outer circle of sixteen lotuses. The lotuses represent the moon, stars, the home and wealth. There are usually other circular designs around the centerpiece. The circles are surrounded by lines on four sides signifying "doors" is called "Bhupur". They symbolize the Earth. The entire painting is adorned at various points with Lakshmi's footprints. Below the Yantra are depicted two puja "asanas" or seats for the couple who perform the puja.

Alternatively, these seats could be meant for the head of the household and the priest who conducts the ceremony. In most Kumaoni households instead of a clay or metal statue of Lakshmi, sugarcane is cut and placed crosswise. Traditional feminine attire like a lahanga (long skirt) and Odhni (shaw!) adorn the sugarcane to make it look like a female form. Thus is the sweetness of life invited with ritual precision to preside over a household.

OTHER ART FORMS

The Shaukas use their own and Tibetan knitting art form to decorate mattresses known as Dans. In these woollen goods we find the mixed influence of the Kumaoni and Tibetan styles. Kumaon also has a distinctive style of making different baskets (Doka, Dala, Tokri); wooden casks (Theki, Harpia, Naliya) for keeping curd, butter and ghee; mattresses (mosta) and ropes etc. The art of Hilljatra mukhotas (masks) is also worth mentioning.

FAIRS AND FESTIVALS

The religious, social and cultural urges of the people of Uttarakhand find an expression in various fairs, which are in turn closely linked to the economic activities of the region. Various folk songs and dances have been kept alive because of these fairs.

In older times, when means of transport were not so good these fairs were an opportunity for friends and relatives to meet regularly. Inspite of all the changes in our society, the tradition of fairs has been kept up by the people. The fairs of Jauljibi, Thal and Bageshwar have been closely linked with the trading activities of the people of this region, while the fairs at Dwarahat, Syalde and Devidhura are important from the religious and cultural point of view.

The fairs and folk festivals of Uttarakhand are very colourful and distinctive, and are the blend of various natural, social and cultural factors. The people of Uttarakhand also celebrate all the major Indian festivals. Basant Panchami, Bhitauli, Harela, Phooldei, Batsavitri, Ganga Dusshera, Dikar Puja, Olgi or Ghee Sankranti, Khatarua, Ghuian Ekadashi and Ghughutia are some of the major festivals of Uttarakhand.

The daily lives of Uttarakhandi women are crowded with a never-ending succession of festivals, most of them involving fasts and the preparation of special foods.

Kumbh Mela: Kumbha (Kumbha means pot) Mela is a sacred Hindu pilgrimage that takes place at the following four locations of India

- Prayag (near the city of Allahabad, in the state of Uttar Pradesh) at the confluence of three rivers Ganga (Ganges), Yamuna and Saraswati
- Haridwar (in the state of Uttar Pradesh) where the river Ganga enters the plains from Himalayas
- Ujjain (in Madhya Pradesh), on the banks of Shipra river, and
- Nasik (in Maharashtra) on the banks of Godavari river.

The pilgrimage occurs four times every twelve years, once at each of the four locations. Each twelve-year cycle includes the Maha (great) Kumbha Mela at Haridwar and Prayag, attended by millions of people, making it the largest pilgrimage gathering around the world.

The observance of Kumbha Mela is based upon the following story : thousands of years ago, perhaps in the Vedic period, gods and demons made a temporary agreement to work together in obtaining amrita (the nectar of immortality) from the Milky Ocean, and to share this equally. However, when the Kumbha (pot) containing the amrita appeared, the demons ran away with the pot and were chased by the gods. For twelve days and twelve nights (equivalent to twelve human years) the gods and demons fought in the sky for the possession of this pot of amrita. It is said that during the battle, drops of amrita fell on to four places : Prayag, Haridwar, Ujjain and Nasik. Thus, Kumbha mela is observed at these four locations where the nectar fell.

Kumbha Mela is attended by millions of people on a single day. A ritual bath at a predetermined time and place is the major event of this festival. Other activities include religious discussions, devotional singing, mass feeding of holy men/women and the poor, and religious assemblies where doctrines are debated and standardized. Kumbha Mela (especially the Maha Kumbha Mela) is the most sacred of all the Hindu pilgrimages. Thousands of holy men/women (monks, saints, sadhus) grace the occasion by their presence. The suspiciousness of Kumbha Mela is in part attributed to the gathering of thousands of holy men/women at one place on earth

The Ardh Kumbh is held every six years and than after six years Kumbh Mela is held. It is said that a holy dip in the river Ganges during the Kumbh & Ardh Kumbh gives you Moksha or Nirvana. According to astrologers, the 'Kumbh Fair' takes place when the planet Jupiter enters Aquarius and the Sun enters Aries.

Jauljibi and Thal Fairs: This fair is held every year in November at Jauljibi, the confluence of the rivers Kali and

Gori, which is a meeting place of three different cultures - the Shauka, the Nepali and the Kumaoni. This gateway to Johar, Darma, Chaudans and Byans was at one time, considered to be the central place between Tibet and the Tarai regions. Though this fair is primarily a commercial one, its cultural importance cannot be overlooked. People come even from Nepal to this fair in order to sell horses, ghee and foreign goods and take back foodgrains, jaggery etc.

A similar fair is held at Thal on Vaishakh Sankranti (14 April) and it attracts a large number of Shaukas. With the closure of the Indo - Tibet trade these fairs have lost their former importance.

The Uttarayani Fair: Uttrayani fair is held in a number of places including Bageshwar, Rameshwar, Sult Mahadev, Chitrashila (Ranibagh) and Hanseshwar etc. on Uttarayani day. At Pancheshwar the dola of Chaumu comes down to the temple. The fair at Bageshwar attracts maximum people. Its commercial, cultural and political importance is still very high. Goods like iron and copper pots, baskets, casks, bamboo articles, mats, mattresses, carpets, blankets, herbs and spices are sold during this fair.

The Uttarayani fairs are often used as platforms by social and political workers and the Bageshwar fair specially has played an important role in all the local movements, as also in the freedom movement. In 1921 activists had given a call for the eventual eradication of the system of bonded labour known as coolie begar. In 1929 Gandhi ji came to Bageshwar. Many freedom fighters and folk singers have been closely associated with the Bageshwar fair. Even today the fair attracts a large number of people, who spend the whole night dancing and singing Jhoras, Chancharis and Bairas.

Nandadevi Fair: The Nandadevi fair is held at Almora, Nainital, Kot (Dangoli), Ranikhet, Bhowali, Kichha and also in the far flung villages of lohar (like Milam and Martoli) and Pindar valleys (like Wachham and Khati). In the villages of the Pindar valley people celebrate the Nanda Devi jaat (journey) every year, while in lohar people come from far and wide to Danadhar, Suring, Milam and Martoli in order to worship the Goddess. In Nainital and Almora thousands take part in the procession carrying the dola (or litter) of Nanda Devi. It is said that the Nanda Devi fairs started in Kumaon during the reign of Kalyan Chand in the 16th Century. A three day fair is held at Kot ki mai or Kot bhramari devi. The fair at Saneti comes every second year. Both these fairs are rich in folk expressions and many village products are brought for sale.

Syalde Bikhauti: It is celebrated on the Vishuwat Sankranti day and commemorates an ancient victory. On this day, the Bagwal is held at Syalde Pokhar in the old town of Dwarahat. People also celebrate the occasion with music, songs and dancing. One day before this a similar fair is held at Vibhandeshwar in which Lord Shiva is worshipped. The Syalde Bikhauti fair has been successful in retaining its old colour and gaiety to a large extent.

Somnath (Masi) Fair: This fair, also on Vishuwat Sankranti day is held in the Shiva temple at Masi. It is a famous fair of Pali Pachhaun. Animals, specially bullocks and calves, are sold at this fair. On the same day a fair is held at Thal. In the summer the people in the valley of Ramganga (West), especially in Masi and Bhikiasen, celebrate the unique machhli utsav (the fish festival). The villagers bearing tumra come with Jaal, fatyav and hathiya to the river to catch fish. The fish festival is locally known as Dahau.

Bagwal—Devidhura Fair: This fair is held in the compound of the Varahi Devi temple at Devidhura on the day of Raksha Bandhan. Devidhura is situated at a trijunction of Almora, Pithoragarh and Nainital districts and the fair is well known for its enchanting folk songs and dances as also for its Bagwal. During the Bagwal the two groups (khams) of people throw stones at each other while they try to protect themselves by using big roof like shields. Even watching the Bagwal is a truly thrilling experience. The Devidhura fair has maintained its old vigour.

Bagwal - Devidhura Fair: This fair is held in the compound of the Varahi Devi temple at Devidhura on the day of Raksha Bandhan. Devidhura is situated at a trijunction of Almora, Pithoragarh and Nainital districts and the fair is well known for its enchanting folk songs and dances as also for its Bagwal. During the Bagwal the two groups (khams) of people throw stones at each other while they try to protect themselves by using big roof like shields. Even watching the Bagwal is a truly thrilling experience. The Devidhura fair has maintained its old vigour.

Jageshwar Fair: This fair is held on the fifteenth day of the month of Baishakh (late March or early April) at the Shiva temple in Jageshwar. During the fair people take holy dips in the Brahma Kund (pool) and worship Lord Shiva. On this day, fairs are also held in many other places.

Purnagiri Fair: Many people throng the temple at Purnagiri, which is situated on the top of a mountain on the right bank of the river Kali near Tanakpur, in the district of Champawat. The temple is very crowded during the Navaratris of Paush and Chaitra. Every year a fair is held on Vishuwat Sankranti and this attracts a large number of pilgrims. After the Holi festival, the longest fair of Kumaon (for about 40 days) starts at Purnagiri. Thousands of people visit the shrine these days.

Haatkalika Fair: On the ashtami (eighth day of the month) of the Chaitra and Bhado, a fair is held in the Kalika temple at Gangolihat. People come with drums and flags to pay homage to Goddess Kalika. On this day, animals are sacrificed and offered to the Goddess. The athwar (eight sacrifices) processions with drums and dances are worth seeing.

Makar Sankranti—Ghugutia: According to the Hindu religious texts, on the day of Uttarayani, the sun enters the Zodiacal sign of 'Makar' (Capricon) from the Zodiacal sign of the Kark (Cancer), i.e. from this day onwards the sun becomes 'Uttarayan' or it starts moving to the north. It is said that from this day, which signals a change of season, the migratory birds start returning to the hills. On Makar Sankranti people give

Khichadi (a mixture of pulses and rice) in charity, take ceremonial dips in holy rivers, participate in the Uttarayani fairs and celebrate the festival of Ghughutia or Kale Kauva.

During the festival of Kale Kauva (literal translation 'black crow') people make sweetmeats out of sweetened flour (flour and gur) deep fried in ghee, shape them like drums, pomegranates, knives, swords etc. They are strung together and worn as necklace-in the middle of which an oragne in fixed. Early in the morning children wear these necklaces and sing "Kale Kauva.." to attract crows and other birds and offer them portions of these necklaces, as a token of welcome for all the migratory birds, who are now coming back after their winter sojourn in the plains.

Wearing garlands of the above eatables the children come out calling the crows with following song on their lips:

Kale Kale, bhol bate aile

bor puwa Khale

Ie Kauva bara, mai ke de sunu gharo

Ie Kauva dhal, mai ke de sunu thai.

(come dear crow, come daily

you will enjoy eating bara and puwa.

Take the bara and give me a pitcher full of gold Take the shield and give me a golden plate).

Basant Panchami: The festival of Basant Panchami celebrates the coming of the spring season. This festival, which also signals the end of winter, is generally celebrated during Magh (January - February). During this festival people worship the Goddess Saraswati, use yellow handkerchiefs or even yellow cloths and in a few places people put a yellow tilak on their foreheads. This festival also marks the beginning of holi baithaks.

Phool Dei: Phool Dei is celebrated on the first day of the month of Chaitra in mid March. On this day, young girls conduct most of the ceremonies. In some places this festival is celebrated throughout the month with the advent of spring.

During this festival young girls go to all the houses in the muhalla or the village with plates full of rice, jaggery, coconut, green leaves and flowers. They offer their good wishes for the prosperity of the household and are given blessings and presents (sweets, gur, money etc) in return.

In a few places even today they sprinkle flowers and rice on the doorsteps and sing:

phool dei, chamma dei

deno dwar, bhur bhakar

yo dei sei namashkar, puje dwar

Sei (a pudding made with floor, curd and jaggery) is prepared specially for this occasion. Folk singers sing the Riturain, Chaiti and other songs welcoming spring and are given presents, money and foodgrains.

Harela and Bhitauli: On the first day of the navaratris (nine day holy period) of the month of Chaitra women fill baskets with soil and sow seven types of grains in them. The grains germinate symbolizing the future harvest. These yellow leaves, called Harela, are cut on the tenth day and people put them on their heads and behind their ears. During the month of Chaitra (March-April) brothers send presents to their sisters. These presents are called Bhitauli.

Harela is peculiarly a Kumaoni festival to mark the advent of the rainy season. The celebration falls on the first day of Shravan. Ten days before the due date, seeds of either five or seven kinds of grains are mixed together and sown in pots inside the room, using small baskets filled with earth. The sowing is done either by the head of the family or the family priest. It is done ceremoniously. Water is sprinkled after worship. On the last day of the month of Aasarh, one day before the actual celebration of the festival, a kind of mock weeding is done with small wooden hoes. Gaily painted images of Shiva and Parvati and their off springs are prepared and worshipped on the Shankranti day. Green shoots Harela are placed on the head gear.

The significance of Harela lies in the fact that it provides an opportunity to the cultivator to test the qualities or defects of the seeds he has in his store. Another significance is that the festival is the occasion to give taken monetary allowances - pocket money to the young girls of the family.

However, the more popular Harela is the one that is celebrated in the month of Shravan to commemorate the wedding of Lord Shiva and Parvati and to welcome the rainy season and the new harvest. On this day people make Dikaras* or clay statues of Gauri, Maheshwar, Ganesh etc. and worship them. Even the overworked bullocks are given a rest on the occasion of Harela. People put the blades of freshly cut Harela on their heads and send them to their relatives and friends as well.

Olgia (Ghee Sankranti): Olgia is celebrated on the first day of Bhado (middle of August), when the harvest is lush and green, vegetables are in abundance and the milch animals very productive. In ancient times sons-in-law and nephews would give presents to fathers-in-law and maternal uncles, respectively, in order to celebrate Olgia. Today agriculturists and artisans give presents to the owners of their land and purchasers of their tools and receive gifts and money in return. Binai (oral harp), datkhocha (metallic tooth pick), metal calipers, axes, ghee, vegetables and firewood are some of the presents exchanged on this day. People put ghee on their foreheads and eat ghee and chapatis stuffed with 'urad' dal. It is believed that walnuts sweeten after this festival. This festival, which is a celebration of the produce of the land, is now seldom celebrated.

Khatarua: Khatarua is essentially the special festival of pastoral- agricultural society and celebrated on the first day of the month of Ashwin in mid September, and signifies the beginning of the autumn. On this day people light bonfires, around which children dance, holding aloft colourful flags. People take special care of their animals and feed them fresh grass. Cucumbers are offered to the fire of Khatarua, which is said to destroy all evil influences. The victory of the king of Kumaon is also said to be one of the reasons for the celebration of Khatarua.

Bat Savitri: This festival is celebrated on the Krishna amavasya (last day of the dark half of the month) of Jyestha and on the day married women worship Savitri and the Bat or banyan tree (Ficus benghalensis) and pray for the well being of their spouses. Women observe fast in honour of Savitri and Satyavan and remember how Savitri through her intense devotion saved her husband from the claws of death.

Ganga Dusshera or Dasar: Ganga Dusshera is celebrated on the Shukla dasami of the Jyestha (May - June). The sacred Ganga is worshipped on this day and Dusshera posters (dwarpatras or dasars), which have various geometric designs on them, are put up on the doors of houses and temples. These posters, once hand written by brahmins, are now printed. On this day people bathe in the holy rivers.

Janopunyu: The people of Kumaon celebrate Raksha Bandhan and Janopunyu, the day on which people change their janeu (sacred thread). On this day the famous Bagwal fair is held at Devidhura in district Champawat.

Nandadevi Rajjaat Yatra: The three week long Nandadevi Rajjaat is one of the world famous festival of Uttarakhand. People from entire Garhwal-Kumaon as well as other parts of India and the world participate in Nandadevi Raj Jat Yatra.

Goddess Nanda Devi is worshipped at dozens of places in Kumaon, but the region around Mt. Nanda Devi and its sanctuary, which falls in the districts of Pithoragarh, Almora and Chamoli, is the prime area related to Nanda Devi.

In Chamoli Nanda Devi Rajjaat is organized once in 12 years. The jaat starts from Nauti village near Karnprayag and goes upto the heights of Roopkund and Haemkund with a four horned sheep. After the havan-yagna is over, the sheep is freed with decorated ornaments, food and clothings and the other offerings are dischared. People also celebrate the annual Nanda jaat.

Though in the Johar region there is no tradition of Nanda Rajjaat but the worship, dance and the ritual of collecting

Brahmkamals (it is called Kaul Kamphu) is part of Nanda festivals.

Chhipla Jaat: Chhiplakot is situated in the heart land of Kali and Gori rivers, south of Panchchuli mountains. The highest point of this mountain - Najurikund (4497m) - is the seat of Chhipla Kedar.

The people of 15 - 20 villages of Dharchula and Gorikhal regions reach Kedardwe and Najurikote every third year (last 2002, next 2005) on Bhado Purnmasi. The principal yatra starts from village Khela near Tawaghat. It goes through thick forests, rocky lands and Bugyals. People go there barefoot even in these days.

The dhami burha or bonia (folk priest) finalizes the dates of the jaat. With folk drums, bhankaras (metallic pipe instrument) and neja (the flag of red cloth pieces collected from all the families of the villages) the jaat goes to Barmano, which is 6 km from Khela. On the second day the yatris go through a thick oak forest. After crossing Bunga, Garapani, Mangthil gwar, Ganbhujdhura (the blooming bugyal) comes Brahmkund (18 km). Around 100 people can stay at the udiyar (cave) of Brahmkund.

From this point one can have a glimpse of Chaudans region and the peaks of W. Nepal. On the third day the route is on the back of Najurikote, which is full of buggi grass and brahmkamals (Saussurea obvallata). At Kedardwe pond sacred dips are taken and the worship is performed. For the night, the yatris have to come back to Brahmkund. On this day one has to trek about 35 km.

On the fourth day after seeing Jyulital and Patojkund the Jaat reaches Bhaiman Kund (16 km). This small lake is like Brahmkund. A night stay is possible in the cave. On the fifth day, one can reach Baram in Gori valley after seeing the Kanar devi temple. If some one wants to remain with the jaat, he can come back to Khela and participate in the village fair.

Chhipla Jaat expresses different aspects of human faith. The bare foot journey, worship, bath, collective food, songs and dances and the possession of the body of Bonia by the folk god are the essential parts of Chhipla Jaat.

Hilljatra: The Hilljatra, which is being celebrated in some parts of Pithoragarh district, is essentially the festival of pastoralists and agriculturalists. In the developmental process, the aathon (eighth day of bhado) and Gawra Visarjan also became the part of Hilljatra. The festival, which basically came to the Sor valley from the Sorar (Mahakali) region of West Nepal, was first introduced in Kumaour village. The Jatra was also accepted by the people of Bajethi, another village near Pithoragarh town and with some modifications it was introduced in Kanalichhina and Askot regions as Hiran chital.

The Hilljatra is related to ropai (the plantation of paddy) and other agricultural and pastoral labours of the rainy season (Hill = mud, Jatra = Jaat). It has also been connected with the victory of the Champawat ruler. There is another story that Kuru, the representative of a Chand King, who went to Sorar (Nepal) to participate in the hilljatra, was able to sacrifice a buffalo with horns covering the neck. The people became happy and wanted to present Kuru a gift.

Kuru thought of introducing this festival in Sor valley and asked for four masks, Lakhiabhoot, Halwaha, two bullocks, and one implement - the Nepali plough. In this way, the hilljatra was introduced in Sor.

In the first part of jatra, worship and the ritual sacrifice of goats is performed, and in the second part, different pastoral and agricultural activities are presented in a dramatic way. The masks are very expressive and this is the most entertaining part of the festival.

In the third and last part, the songs are recited with the performance of circle dance (Chanchari). It continues late into the night. The songs are traditional as well as new and popular. The hilljatra is a living tradition and all care should be taken to preserve its style in a rapidly changing society.

Kandali: In the Chaudans region of Pithoragarh district, a flower - Kandali (Strobilenthes wallichii) - blooms once every

12 years (last in 1999) and the people celebrate Kandali festival between the months of August and October. The Chaundas Valley is remote in the Dharchula tehsil of Pithoragarh. It lies between the Kali and the Dhauli rivers. In the week long festival the local people - Shaukas or the Rangs participate with gaiety and enthusiasm in different villages of the region. Some stories are associate with this festival, which express the martial tradition of the Shaukas.

In the first story, it is said that by tasting the poisonous flower of the Kandali the only son of a widow died. In the second story, this flower the symbol of famine and poverty. According to the third and most popular story, the region was once attacked while the menfolk were away for trade. The brave women repelled the enemy, who hid in the Kandali bushes, and the attacked the bushes and destroyed the enemy. The festival commemorates their bravery and the women therefore destroy the plant ceremonially to remind the local people of the incident and to prevent further mishaps.

The festival begins with the worship of a Shiva Linga made of barley and buck wheat flour mixture. Local liquor is traditionally used during this festival. Every household performs it in a decorated comer of the courtyard. People pray for prosperity. The individual pujas are followed by a community feast. Then, the women and men, in their traditional dresses and laden with gold and silver ornaments, assemble around a tree on the sacred ground of the village. Strips of white cloth are tied to the tree and a flag is raised.

A procession is formed behind the flag. The women lead the procession, each armed with a ril (an implement used in compacting carpet on the loom) followed by children and men armed with swords and shields. As they sing and dance their music echoes in the valley.

On approaching the blooms, war like tunes are played and war cries uttered and the women attack the bushes with their rils. The menfolk then come to their aid, and the bushes are hacked with swords. They uproot the bushes and take them back as the spoils of the war. Victory cries are raised and rice grains are again cast towards the sky to honour the deities with the prayer that the people of Chaundas Valley may be ever victorious over enemies. Festivity, dancing and music continue throughout the night.

The enthusiasm and emotion have to be seen to be believed. All the members of the community, even those living elsewhere, return to their village for the event, on the return of the procession to the village an assembly known as the 'Savdhoomo-sabha' is held at which sweetmeats, liquor and fruits are consumed, the deities are again worshipped with flowers. Festivity, dancing and music continue throughout the night.

Uttarakhandi Holi (Kumaoni Holi): The uniqueness of the Kumaoni Holi lies in its being a musical affair, whichever may be its form, be it the Baithki Holi, the Khari Holi or the Mahila Holi. The Baithki Holi and Khari Holi are unique in that the songs on which they are based have touch of melody, fun and spiritualism. These songs are essentially based on classical ragas. No wonder then the Baithki Holi is also known as Nirvan Ki Holi.

The Baithki Holi begins from the premises of temples, where Holiyars (the professional singers of Holi songs) as also the people gather to sing songs to the accompaniment of classical music.

Kumaonis are very particular about the time when the songs based on ragas should be sung. For instance, at noon the songs based on Peelu, Bhimpalasi and Sarang ragas are sung while evening is reserved for the songs based on the ragas like Kalyan, Shyamkalyan and Yaman etc.

The Khari Holi is mostly celebrated in the rural areas of Kumaon. The songs of the Khari Holi are sung by the people, who sporting traditional white churidar payajama and kurta, dance in groups to the tune of ethnic musical instruments.

10

Education

EDUCATION IN UTTARAKHAND

Education in Uttarakhand is provided by a large number of public and private institutions. Uttarakhand had a long tradition of learning and culture.

On 30 September 2010 there were 15,331 primary schools with 1,040,139 students and 22,118 working teachers. At the 2011 census the literacy rate of the state was 78.81% with 87.4% literacy for males and 70% literacy for females. The language of instruction in the schools is either English or Hindi. There are mainly government-run, private unaided (no government help), and private aided schools in the state. The main school affiliations are CBSE, CISCE or UBSE, the state syllabus defined by the Department of Education of the Government of Uttarakhand.

Uttarakhand is also home to a number of universities and degree colleges. Dehradun is known as school capital of India.

Detail

In Uttarakhand there are 15,331 primary schools with 1,040,139 students and 22,118 working teachers (Year 2011). Literacy rate of the state was 79.63% with 88.33% literacy for males and 70.70% literacy for females. The language of instruction in the schools is either English or Hindi.

Main building of The Doon School

There are mainly government and private schools and institutions including primary schools, high schools, inter college, degree colleges and technical institutions. The main school affiliations are CBSE, CISCE or the State Government syllabus defined by the Department of Education of the Government of Uttarakhand.

Notable schools and Institutions

There are many notable schools and institutions in Uttarakhand.

- The Doon School Dehradun
- Sherwood College, Nainital
- The Woodstock School Mussoorie
- Oak Grove School (Mussoorie, Uttarakhand), Mussoorie
- St George's College, Mussoorie
- Colonel Brown Cambridge School Dehradun
- Convent of Jesus and Mary, Waverley, Mussoorie
- Wynberg Allen School, Mussoorie

- St Joseph's College, Nainital
- Birla Vidya Mandir, Nainital
- Welham Girls' School, Dehradun
- Welham Boys' School, Dehradun
- St Joseph's Academy, Dehradun
- Lal Bahadur Shastri National Academy of Administration, Mussoorie
- Forest Research Institute, Dehradun
- Indira Gandhi National Forest Academy (IGNFA), Dehradun
- Wildlife Institute of India Dehradun
- Indian Military Academy, Dehradun.

EDUCATIONAL AND RESEARCH INSTITUTIONS

The Schools: For well over a century, Nainital has been known for its many schools. Four schools from the British period continue to exist today: Sherwood College , established 1867; All Saints' College, established 1869; St. Mary's Convent High School established 1878; and St. Joseph's College established 1888. In addition, a number of new schools have been established since independence: Birla Vidyamandir , established 1947; Sanwal School, established in the 1940s in Mallital; Sainik School, established 1966; St. Amtuls Public School, established 1983; Parvati Sah Prema Jagati Saraswati Vihar, established 1983; and Oakwood School, established 1989.

KUMAON UNIVERSITY

Nainital is home to one of the two campuses of Kumaon University (the other being Almora). The university was founded in 1973 when it incorporated the Dan Singh Bisht (DSB) Government College (commonly called "the Degree College"), which had been founded in 1951, with the mathematician Dr. A.N. Singh as its first principal.

ARIES (State Observatory): The 50-year old State Observatory at Nainital was reborn in 2004 as ARIES, the

Aryabhatta Research Institute of Observational-Sciences, an autonomous institute under the Department of Science and Technology, Govt. of India. The Observatory, which had come into existence in Varanasi in 1954, was moved the following year to Nainital, under its more transparent skies. In 1961 it was moved once again to its present location—Manora Peak (altitude 1951 m.) —a few km south of the Nainital town. ARIES's main objective is to provide national optical observing facilities for research in astronomy, astrophysics, and the atmospheric sciences.

Universities and College

Kumaon Engineering Collegelogo

Established	April 21, 1991
Type	Engineering College
Undergraduates	720
Postgraduates	105
Location	Almora, Uttarakhand, India

The Kumaon Engineering College or KEC, is an autonomous engineering and technology institute in the Almora district in state of Uttarakhand established with the sole purpose of imparting technological advances to the state. Established in 1991 the college has travelled 15 years journey, and seen many facelift till date. The institute is fully financed by the government of Uttarakhand and managed by the Board of Governors with the Minister of Technical Education Govt. of Uttarakhand, as the Chairman and Secretary of Technical Education as Vice-Chairman. Principal is the member Secretary of Board of Governors.

The Location: The College is situated in the hilly region of Dwarahat on Kathgodam-Ranikhet-Karnprayag National Highway (87-E), about 30 km. from Ranikhet. The nearest railway station is at Kathgodam (118Km).

The College is spread over an area of 155 Acres at an altitude of 1450 meters. A quiet, congenial, hilly and pollution free environment with a picturesque view surrounding the campus. The summer is pleasant with a max of 30 °C for a few weeks and for rest of the time, the weather remains cool.

The Institute: Kumaon Engineering College is affiliated to Kumaon University Nainital, which imparts technical education to the students. KEC is affiliated to Kumaon University which providest the student with the degrees in the following discipline:

- Bachelor of Engineering in Computer Science
- Bachelor of Engineering in Electronic Engineering
- Bachelor of Engineering in Mechanical engineering
- Bachelor of Engineering in Biochemical Engineering
- Master of Computer Applications

Apart from all these Undergraduate & Postgraduate courses, the college also provides the students with the CCNA and Oracle (scheduled) courses.

The Departments: The College is divided into six departments, which are as follows:

- Applied Science Department
- Computer Science Department
- Electronics Department
- Mechanical Department
- Biochemical Department
- Administration Department

Applied Science Department

- Engineering Chemistry Lab.
- Organic & Physical Chemistry Lab.
- Soil& Water Pollution Lab.
- General Physics Lab.
- Optics Lab

Computer Science Department

The CS department imparts the excellence and innovation to the student of CS and MCA with the Hardware & Software

Labs along with the Computer Centre and VSAT Internet connection (128 KBPS) through DOE, ERNET Project. The department has:

- MS DOS/ Unix Lab.
- Windows NT / Netware Lab.
- Internet lab (Under Linux).
- Internet lab (Under Windows).
- Visual Basic Programming Lab.
- Linux Lab.
- Oracle Lab.

Every year, bright and innovative projects come up on variety of fields including Open GL, linux, Oracle etc.

Electronics Department: This department has the state of art labs relating to electrical & electronics. The following labs are developed with latest equipments.

- Communications Lab.
- Microprocessor Lab.
- Measurements & Instrumentation Lab.
- Basic Electrical Engineering Lab.
- Control System Lab.
- Digital Electronics Lab.
- Power Electronics Lab.
- Discrete Integrated Circuit Lab.
- Electrical Machine Lab.
- PCB Lab.
- Microwave Lab.
- Optical Fiber Lab.

Mechanical Department

The Department has the centralised workshop which works as the umberella for the various other labs related to mechanical engineering. The labs facilitated in the central workshop are as:

- Carpentry Shop.
- Black Smithy Shop.
- FittingShop.
- MachineShop.
- WeldingShop.
- Sheet Metal Shop

The other mechanical department labs include:

- Mechanics lab
- Engineering Drawing lab
- Fluid Mechanics lab

Biochemical Department

This department is in its developing phase and some of the Labs have been developed and some are under development process. It has the following labs:

- Bio Chemistry Lab.
- Life Science Lab.
- Microbiology Lab.
- Chemical Engineering Operations Lab.
- Genetics Lab (planned).
- Industrial Fermentation Lab.
- Computer Aided Design Lab.
- Waste Water Treatment Lab.

Library

The Library is life line of the college. It contains more than 5000 articles and journals, which includes all the books covered by the syllabus, and other technical journal like IEEE and other magzines, varying from computers to human sciences. The library has shifted to its new building just five years back and is still on its way to become a state of art library. The College has a Central Library, which operates on an open access basis. Students and staff members have an access to large number of books and journals, besides large number of competitive and technical magazines. Presently the library is procuring about 14 international journals & 50 national journals.

Library has the latest Library Management Software i.e. LIBSYS for library automation purpose. The catalogue data entry work has been completed and the computerized service (i.e. OPAC) and circulation will be implemented soon. Library is also institutional member of DELNET. The library users are licensed to use the DELNET database for their study / project work / research purpose. Digital library is indeed in process of installation. The library is being further strengthened with large number of books and journals. Software library with latest software also plays a significant role. In the software library any student can use the software. Presently the library is equipped with the following software:

- Multi Sim - 10 User - Electronics Workbench.
- Ultiboard - 10 User - Electronics Workbench.
- ACTIVEHDL - VHDL - 10 User - ALDEC.
- ACTIVEHDL - Verilog - 10 User - ALDEC.
- Synplify - Floating - Synplicity.
- Auto CAD Inventor Series 10 - 5 User
- Comm Sim - 10 User - Electronics Workbentch.
- PCADD - 5 User - Antenna Design.
- PSIM - 5 User.
- Proctus VSM - 25 User.
- NetSim - 10 User.
- ESPRITCAM Computer Added Manufacturing - 5 User

Training and Placement: Training & Placement was the major concern of the students since the college was established. And it was after 10 years the formal creation of Placement cell came into existence. But even after its creation, the body lacked the efficiency. But after 4 years they were able to bring up few big names into the institute, which included Bajaj Auto, HCL Technologies, Satyam Computers and Syntel. Now a separate Training and Placement Cell is being established at Dehradun.

Hostels: The College has 10, boys and girls hostels of different capacities and one transit hostel. One boys hostel (180 single seated) is under construction. The following are the hostels in KEC

- Aravali Hostel [90 X 2] BE First Year (Boys)
- Trishul Hostel [25 X 2] [Owner Of Trishul Hostel- 2005 Passout Batch (Trishul Walon Ka..)]
- Nanda Devi Hostel [60 X 3] BE Second Year (Boys)
- Shivalik Hostel [30 X 2] Second/Final Year (Boys)
- Gaumukh Hostel [60 X 3] BE Third Year (Boys)
- Gangotri Hostel [60 X 3] BE 1st, 2nd, 3rd Year (Girls)
- Kailash Hostel [120 X 1] BE Final Year (Boys)
- Yamunotri Hostel [60 X 2] MCA & BE Final Year (Girls)
- Nalanda Hostel [60 X 1] Adhoc Lecturers Transit Hostel [60 X 1]

UNIVERSITY OF ROORKEE

The Roorkee College was established in 1847 as the First Engineering College in India. The College was renamed as The Thomson College of Civil Engineering in 1854. It was given the status of University by Act No. IX of 1948 of the United Province (Uttar Pradesh) in recognition of its performance and its potential and keeping in view the needs of post-independent India. Pandit Jawahar Lal Nehru, the first Prime Minister of India, presented the Charter in November 1949 elevating the erstwhile college to the First Engineering University of Independent India.

Since its establishment, the University of Roorkee has played a vital role in providing the technical manpower and know-how to the country and in pursuit of research. The University ranked amongst the best technological institutions in the world and has contributed to all sectors of technological development. It has also been considered a trend-setter in the area of education and research in the field of science, technology, and engineering. The University entered 150th year of its existence in one or other form in October 1996.

On the 21 September 2001, the University was declared an institute of national importance, by passing a bill in the parliament, changing its status from University of Roorkee to Indian Institute of Technology Roorkee. Thus another jewel was added into the already glittering crown in the History of this Institute.

Bachelor's Degree courses are offered in 10 disciplines in Engineering and Architecture; 55 Postgraduate Degree courses are offered in Engineering, Applied Science and Architecture and planning. The Institute has facility for doctoral work in all Departments and Research Centres.

The IIT admits students to B.Tech. and B.Arch. courses through the IIT-JEE. conducted at various centres all over India.

University of Roorkee has been instrumental in creating the engineering pool in India during the British rule when engineering education was introduced in just few commonwealth countries. Started with a vision of providing engineering support in the development & maintenance of Ganga Canal, this pioneer institute has become one of the most elite technical institute in India.

WILDLIFE INSTITUTE OF INDIA

Wildlife Institute of India (WII), Government of India is an internationally renowned premiere institution in India run by the Indian Council of Forestry Research and Education which trains wildlife managers and wildlife researchers.

Trained personnel from WII have contributed immensely in studying and protecting the Wildlife of India. WII has popularized wildlife studies and careers in India.

The institute is based in Dehradun India. It is located in Chandrabani, which is close to the southern forests of Dehradun.

The Indian Council of Forestry Research and Education also runs the Forest Research Institute, The Indian Forest Service and the Indian Institute of Forest Management.

EDUCATION OF SCHOOL

Uttarakhand has been the centre of education from the ancient time. It is believed that the Kauravas and Pandavas were trained by Guru Dronacharya in the foothills of Himalaya that's why Dehradun is also known as Drona Nagari.

India's best schools and training institutes are located in Uttarakhand - FRI, IIT Roorkee, Wadia Institute of Himalayan Geology, Indian Institute of Petroleum, Survey of India, Indian Military Academy, Wildlife Institute of India, L.B.S. National Academy of Administration, Indian Institute of Remote Sensing, Doon School, Sherwood College, Rashtriya Indian Military College, Nehru Institute of Mountain-eeringare a few to name.

Uttarakhand was ranked 3rd in "Education Development and Achievement, at Elementary Level, in India" in a survey conducted in August 2005 by India Today.

Education in the state of Uttarakhand has a sound background, right from the inception of the state department of education is running ahead and getting shape gradually.

SAINIK SCHOOL GHORAKHAL

Mission Statement: Sainik School, Ghorakhal aims at preparing its students for the officers cadre in the Armed Forces and for various other responsible positions in all walks of life.

Background: Sainik School, Ghorakhal is a residential school providing public school education. It was established on 21 March 1966. The School was established in Ghorakhal Estate of the Nawab of Rampur near Bhowali in Nainital District.

Campus: The school is situated at an altitude of about 6,000 feet above mean sea level amidst idyllic surroundings of the Kumaon Hills, from Bhowali approximately 2.5 kms and it has famous temple of GOLLU DEVTA. It has a salubrious climate which is quite conducive to studies as well as games, sports and other co-curricular activities. This school is exclusively meant for boys between the age group of 10 to 11 years. The

School started with approximately 60 students divided in two houses SINGH and KESARI.

The first Principal was Wg Cdr. Jaimal Singh, first Registrar was Sqd Ldr. P N Khanna and Head Mater Major T C Mehta. Among the first teaching staff were Mr. Ramesh Chandra Srivastava teaching History, Mr. Vaidya Bhushan Pant teaching English and Table Tennis, Mr. Om Parkash Gupta teaching Mathematics Mr. Noor Mohammed teaching NCC/Arts and Craft and fond of hunting in the forest hills around the school.

Mr. K S Chhikara was the first Physical Training instructor who with his hard work and earlier career in Indian Navy looked after all the sports and physical activities, on Saturday morning he used to give the moral lecture about the practical and future life of the baby and budding military officers. The school has produced excellent officers for the Indian armed forces (army/navy and IAF) and those who can not due to some reason make it to Defence Services have done extremely well in civil life as Doctors/Engineers/Scientist/Administrative services and many have even ventured out and turned out to be successful in businesses.

Atmosphere: Boys are prepared academically, physically and mentally for entry into National Defence Academy (NDA).

Sports: Hockey, cricket, athletics, football, table tennis, basketball and volleyball are the principal games. Cross country and boxing are the other main attractions.

Extra Curricular Activities: There are a number of clubs for the students. A Radio Club, Photography Club, English and Hindi Debating Club and a Gardening Club to enrich the life of the school.

Bibliography

Bahadur, Prasad, Lal : *Indian Political System and Law*, New Delhi, Shree, 2005.

Baird, Robert: *Religion in Modern India*, New Delhi, Manohar, 1981.

Basham, A.L.: *A Cultural History of India*, Oxford, Clarendon Press, 1975.

Desai, Mahadev : *Gandhi and Indian Villages*, New Delhi, Mohit Pub., 2002.

Frauwallner, E..: *History of Indian Philosophy*, Motilal, Delhi, 1973.

Grisenold, H.D.: *Insights into Modern Hinduism*, Oxford, New York, 1934.

Kalika Prasad Tiwari: *Foundations of Ancient Indian Culture*, Pointer Publishers, Delhi, 2001.

Krishna Murari: *The Calukyas of Kalyani, from circa 973 A.D. to 1200 A.D.*, Delhi, Concept, 1977.

Krishna Rao M. V.; *Studies in Kautilya*, Munshiram Manoharlal, Delhi, 1979.

Levinson, D.: *Family Violence in Cross Cultural Perspective*, Newbury Park, Sage, 1989.

Macdonell, Arthur A: *Vedic Index of Names and Subjects.* London: Murray, 1912.

Mayer, A.: *Caste in an Indian Village: Change and Continuity 1954-1992*, Delhi, OUP, 1996.

Metcalf, Thomas R.: *Modern India: An Interpretive Anthology*, London, Macmillan, 1971.

Misra, Satya Swarup: *The Aryan Problem: A Linguistic Approach*, Munshiram Manoharlal, New Delhi, 1992.

Mookerjee R. R.: *Local Government in Ancient India*, Oxford University Press, 1920.

Parel , J.: *Hind Swaraj or Indian Home Rule*, Cambridge University Press, 1925.

Possehl, Gregory L.: *The Harappan Civilization*, London, Aris and Phillips, 1982.

Prahlad K.: *Governance and Public Administration for Poverty Reduction*, Salvador, Brazil, 1997.

Prasad, Lal Bahadur : *Indian Political System and Law*, New Delhi, Shree, 2005.

Richard Davis: *Lives of Indian Images,* Princeton Univ. Press. Princeton, 1997.

Rosenblum, G.: *Law as a Political Instrument,* New York, Random House, 1955.

Schwartz, Cowan, Ruth: *A Social History of American Technology.* New York: Oxford University Press, 1996.

Seyla Benhabib: *The Reluctant Modernism of Hannah Arendt*, Rowan and Littlefield Publishers, 2003.

Shani, G.: *Communalism, Caste and Hindu Nationalism: The Violence in Gujarat*, Cambridge Univ Press, Delhi, 2003.

Shashipriya Dei: *Development of Temple Architecture in India*, Punthi-Pustak, Delhi, 1998.

Simon, D. : *Public Administration,* New York, Knopf, 1950.

Singh, Harbans: *The Heritage of the Sikhs*, Columbia, Missouri, South Asia Books, 1983.

Singh, M.N.: *Fundamentals of Indian Culture: A Modernistic View of Ancient Traditions*, Pratibha Prakashan, Delhi, 2010.

Sivaramamurti, C.: *Sri Lakshmi in Indian Art and Thought*, Kanak, New Delhi, 1982.

Sri Aurobindo: *The Foundations of Indian Culture*, Pondicherry, 1980.

Subhan, John A.: *Sufism: Its Saints and Shrines*, Lucknow, 1938.

Susan Huntington: *The Art of Ancient India,* Weatherhill, 1985.

Uphoff, N.: *Local Organizations: Intermediaries in Rural Development*, Ithaca, Cornell University Press, 1984.

Victor G. : *Law as a Political Instrument,* New York, Random House, 1955.

Wheare, Kenneth C. : *Modern Constitutions*, New York, Oxford University Press, 1951.

Zelermyer, William (1977). *The Legal System in Operation.* St. Paul, MN: West Publishing.

Index